SUPER
NATURAL
DESTINY

D1377600

DESTINY IMAGE PRODUCTS
BY DON NORI, SR.

BOOKS
The Angel and the Judgment
Breaking Generational Curses
The Love Shack
Manifest Presence
The Prayer God Loves to Answer
*Romancing the Divine Secrets of
the Most Holy Place, Volumes 1 & 2*
Tales of Brokenness
You Can Pray in Tongues
Breaking Demonic Strongholds
Yes, the Prayer God Loves to Answer
So You Want to Change the World?

VIDEO
The Dream and the Church, DVD
Freedom From Guilt, DVD
Introduction to the Most Holy Place, DVD

AUDIO
A Deeper Walk Through the Temple, CD
How to Give Yourself to His Presence, CD
Inside the Holy of Holies, CD
Walk Through the Temple, CD

AVAILABLE FROM DESTINY IMAGE PUBLISHERS

14.99

Presented To:

_____

From:

_____

Date:

_____

DON NORI, SR.

SUPER
NATURAL
DESTINY

ANSWERING GOD'S CALL
ON YOUR LIFE

DESTINY IMAGE® PUBLISHERS, INC.

P.O. Box 310, Shippensburg, PA 17257-0310

"Promoting Inspired Lives."

This book and all other Destiny Image, Revival Press, MercyPlace, Fresh Bread, Destiny Image Fiction, and Treasure House books are available at Christian bookstores and distributors worldwide.

For a U.S. bookstore nearest you, call 1-800-722-6774.

For more information on foreign distributors, call 717-532-3040.

Reach us on the Internet: www.destinyimage.com.

ISBN 13 TP: 978-0-7684-4017-1

ISBN 13 Ebook: 978-0-7684-8923-1

ISBN Audio: 978-0-7684-0271-1

For Worldwide Distribution, Printed in the U.S.A.

1 2 3 4 5 6 7 8

Dedication

This book is dedicated to dreamers everywhere. Never give up. Trust what you cannot see, believe what no one else can hear, and do what no one else has done.

Endorsements

Loving God, hearing His voice, and persevering through every demonic obstacle is the purpose of life. As you read Don Nori, Sr.'s book, *Supernatural Destiny*, I believe the same supernatural anointing that allowed him to fulfill his destiny will splash on you.

Sid Roth, Host
It's Supernatural! Television
www.SidRoth.org

How God led Don Nori, Sr., to begin Destiny Image is an amazing story. I can't wait to read how God continued to guide Don through the years to be faithful to publish what was on the heart of God. I believe this will be a very interesting book. I thank God for Don and Destiny Image.

Randy Clark
Founder of the Apostolic Network of Global Awakening
Evangelist and Author
www.GlobalAwakening.com

Great men or women of God are defined by the shadow they cast. To cast a shadow one has to stand in the light, and others must embrace that same light. Don Nori, Sr., casts a giant shadow that secures his lineage and legacy as a man who hears God's voice. I have been blessed and greatly impacted by the vision of this dear man of God and am thankful to have crossed the light of his path. With this view in mind, I commend to you the pilgrimage and journey of this pioneer. As you read this book, perhaps you too will be impacted by the faith, hope, and love that rests upon this champion's life.

James W. Goll
Encounters Network, Prayer Storm, Compassion Acts
Author of *The Seer*, *The Lost Art of Intercession*, *Prayer Storm*, and *Dream Language*
www.encountersnetwork.com

Trace the supernatural journey of the founding and expansion of Destiny Image, which has provided a channel for God's voice to be heard throughout the world. I believe you will also discover keys to unlock your God-given purpose through the wisdom Don Nori, Sr., has gathered.

Ché Ahn
Senior Pastor, HROCK Church, Pasadena, CA
International Chancellor, Wagner Leadership Institute
President, Harvest International Ministry

Don Nori, Sr., has always been a history-maker. I clearly remember the early days of Destiny Image, when the office for the publishing company was in the living room of his house. He and Cathy were deeply and totally committed to publishing the prophets in response to a clear and compelling call from the Lord that was revealed by way of a series of visions Don received while driving on the interstate. While the vision solidified Don's commitment to the call, the hand of the Lord had been on Don long before that in terms of his prophetic gift. His heart to see the Body of Christ embrace the fullness of what the Lord is saying and doing has never changed. His determination to release the writings of prophetic voices to the ends of the earth is now clearly history! The early days of Destiny Image were both challenging and exciting, and those of us whom Don allowed to listen in on his conversations with the Lord were all deeply impacted by Don's clarity of vision and his depth of commitment to the heart of the Father.

As you read this story of Don's journey, realize that you are reading the story of a history-maker, a true prophet of the Lord who carries a history-making word that shapes and reshapes the landscape of the Kingdom. As you read this story of one man's journey toward becoming a history-maker, may it awaken the history-maker in you. May you be willing to obey the Lord in your sphere and measure of rule as Don has done in his. History-makers don't arrive on the scene for a small price; the cost is quite great. I have counted it a great privilege to know Don and to have worked with him from those early days of small beginnings, even until these marvelous days of global impact. Blessed are the history-makers!

Dr. Mark J. Chironna
Senior Pastor, The Master's Touch International Church
Orlando, Florida
www.markchironna.com

In a strategic hour for the Church, Don Nori, Sr., had a call from God to help hear and publish the quickened word of God for this present age. Destiny Image Publishing emerged from this anointed vision, and millions of lives have been enlightened, transformed, and encouraged as a result. For my wife and me, it has been a special joy to share a small portion of the journey with this great publishing house and its anointed team. We believe its greatest days are yet to come!

Mahesh Chavda
Chavda Ministries International
www.maheshchavda.com

I know Don to be a true pioneer. He is a man of the Presence and committed to advancing the Kingdom. Don is a man of passion and integrity. I love the story of Destiny Image!

Todd Bentley
Fresh Fire Ministries
www.freshfireusa.com

The title of this book *Supernatural Destiny* is the perfect description of the miracle of Destiny Image being willing to publish my book (*Lady in Waiting*). The book had been turned down by some 20 publishers over a 5-year period. Destiny Image took a chance on *Lady in Waiting,* and the rest is history—translated into some 14 languages and a best seller for more than 15 years. Destiny Image listened to the "holy nudge" of God, and a "supernatural destiny" happened not only in relation to *Lady in Waiting* but also to a national speaking ministry that burst forth from the success of the book.

Jackie Kendall
Best-selling author of *Lady in Waiting*
President of Power to Grow Ministry
www.JackieKendall.com

I have known Don Nori, Sr., for over twenty-five years. I was there with him before there was a Destiny Image. I was there when Heaven unveiled his future. I was there when Don said "yes" to that future in spite of the great cost he would have to endure for following his supernatural destiny.

William Jennings Bryan said that destiny is no matter of chance. It is a matter of choice. It is not a thing to be waited for; it is a thing to be achieved. Don made a decision in those days that would bless the whole world.

Supernatural Destiny is Don's story, but it is also your story. With the pen of a prophetic writer, Don encourages us to embrace our own destiny and reminds us that we never walk alone as we follow the dreams God has planted in our spirits. Thank you, Don, for this book. You have always been a great inspiration to me and an inspiration to thousands of people around the world. I am blessed to be counted as one of your friends.

Don Milam
VP, Author Development
Destiny Image Publishers
www.destinyimage.com

Don Nori's new book is a story that brings to life all the lessons of maturing faith. He is a master storyteller and knows how to father others through the tale of his own gripping journey and career. In some ways, you are getting the depth of a thousand books in one because of his experience in the publishing arena. Thank God for his life of sacrifice; you will benefit from it in this powerful new book!

Shawn Bolz
Author of *Keys to Heaven's Economy* and
The Nonreligious Guide to Dating and Being Single
Director/Pastor of Expression58 in Hollywood, California
www.expression58.org

Don Nori, Sr., is a prophet. But, Don is more than a prophet; he is a modern-day mystic. He is a visionary author and renowned publisher. He is a man who pursues the heart of God with sincere passion. In a powerful visitation, Don was overshadowed by the presence of the Holy Spirit. Don felt the heavens open, and his ears were tuned to hear the heartbeat of God. The near-audible voice of the Lord issued a mandate, "Publish My prophets!" Don humbly answered God's call to make God's treasures known to the generations. With tears running down his face, he conceived Destiny Image Publishers. Within the power-packed pages of *Supernatural Destiny*, you will find valuable keys to help unlock your own life's dream and destiny call. *Supernatural Destiny* will inspire you to pay the price to fulfill your own unique call to destiny and godly purpose upon the earth.

Barbie L. Breathitt
Breath of the Spirit Ministries, Inc.
www.BarbieBreathitt.com
www.MyOnar.com (Dream Interpretation Website)
Author of *Dream Encounters: Seeing Your Destiny From God's Perspective, So You Want to Change the World?*, *Hearing and Understanding the Voice of God,* and *Power Over the Impossible*, Destiny Image Publishers

Don Nori, Sr., relates an adventure in the Lord that lavishes hope to everyone with a dream and a word from the Lord. Untold millions have benefited from his obedience to publish and distribute the word of God to the entire earth.

After reading *Supernatural Destiny,* you will have courage to follow through with your divine purpose.

Randy DeMain
Kingdom Revelation Ministries
www.kingdomrevelation.org

Contents

Foreword
by Dr. Myles Munroe

This eloquent and immensely thought-provoking work gets to the heart of how to discover and pursue your destiny.

This is indispensable reading for anyone who wants to live life above the norm and learn the principle of fulfilling destiny. This is a profound authoritative work which spans the vision of a man moved by the passion of his call. This book is filled with wisdom that breaks new ground in its approach and will possibly become a classic in this and the next generation.

This exceptional work by my friend Don Nori, Sr., is one of the most profound, practical, principle-centered approaches to this subject of fulfilling your dream I have read in a long time. The author's approach to this timely issue brings a fresh breath of air that captivates the heart, engages the mind, and inspires the spirit of the reader.

The author's ability to leap over theological jargon and reduce complex theories to simple, practical principles that the least among us can understand is amazing. This work will challenge the intellectual while embracing the layman, delivering profound truths with simplicity.

Don's approach awakens in the reader the untapped inhibitors that retard our personal development, and his antidotes empower us to rise above these self-defeating, self-limiting factors to a life of exploits in spiritual and mental advancement. This book inspires you to believe that nothing is impossible.

The author also integrates into each chapter time-tested precepts, giving each principle a practical application to life that makes the entire process people-friendly.

Every sentence of this book is pregnant with wisdom, inspiration, and prophetic insight; I enjoyed the mind-expanding experience of this exciting work. I admonish you to plunge into this ocean of knowledge and watch your life change for the better.

Dr. Myles Munroe
President and Chairman
BFM International
ITWLA
Nassau, Bahamas

Foreword
by Paula White

We have been in times of incredible change and unparalleled opportunity that have pushed us to the far reaches of our faith. As the world around us experiences ongoing flux and instability, believers are facing challenging situations that may leave them wondering what God's plans for their lives are. They often question when, and if, their God-designed destiny will reveal itself—and how it can truly come to pass amid so much uncertainty and turmoil.

These pressing questions are what make Don Nori's book, *Supernatural Destiny,* so vital, inspirational, and prophetic for these times. The story of how Don received his God-given vision while driving along a highway—a vision that would birth the life-transforming publishing ministry of Destiny Image—truly exemplifies God's plan for our lives at work.

When God chose Don to fulfill the role of "a prophet to publish prophets," He selected a man who was simply going about his everyday life—fulfilling the call of God on his life as a pastor while dutifully taking caring of his family with a "day job." God saw a man who was already in his purpose—not yet walking out the greater blueprint the Lord had to show him—but a man who had already committed to walk with Him...and who was positioned, aligned, and prepared for his next mission.

Supernatural Destiny reveals how one man's obedience to walk out the plan of God, on faith, has returned a fertile harvest impacting countless lives...and how, more than 25 years later, Destiny Image has become the vibrant, productive, prospering publishing house of some of the most powerful, revelation-filled, and life-transforming Christian resources on the market today.

When the desperate, the lonely, the dejected, the ill, the fearful, and the forgotten have needed to receive encouragement, Destiny Image has fulfilled its vision to publish authors with "an anointing to direct, encourage, and strengthen" their readers—by illustrating and testifying to the life-transforming power of God's love.

Today, when Christian believers need guidance and strategies to help them navigate the overwhelming myriad of viewpoints, platforms, technologies, and outlets of information—*and disinformation*—Destiny Image resources counterbalance and combat this onslaught of confusion, offering biblically sound applications for dealing with today's real world issues and challenges.

Don's "ear to hear" the Word of the Lord prepared Him to receive, and act on, the vision God delivered. In his willingness to step out on faith…his willingness to believe that what God was showing him was real…his willingness to sacrifice his very home during Destiny Image's humble beginnings, Don models the kind of acceptance, humility, perseverance, and commitment God looks for to bring His will—*and our divine purpose*—to fruition.

Supernatural Destiny will give you insight into how to hear from God and apply your faith to your daily walk as you go through the life processes God uses to transform us into the vessels that will carry out His will on earth.

I pray that you will be inspired by Don Nori's powerful story of how God reached down and "touched" him—and that you, too, will begin to prepare yourself *on faith* to experience God's *Supernatural Destiny* in your life!

Paula White
Senior Pastor
Without Walls International Church

Introduction

Many writers like to save the best news till the end of the book. They say that is the best way to get folks to read through the entire book. But I have a different plan. I want to give you the best news in the very beginning.

God has a plan for your life. He has dreamed a dream for you that only you can fulfill. He holds that dream in His heart, working daily in your life in order to bring you to the place where everything He has dreamed for you can come to pass.

Here is some more good news. Even if you feel that you have failed Him, He still holds His plan for you in His heart. He still loves you. He is still determined to give you the best life possible. He is still determined to bring about His incredible dreams for your life.

Your level of faith is not the issue. What matters is that your heart is open to Jesus. He will fulfill His destiny for you not based on what church you go to, but on your availability to Him. The world is full of unfulfilled dreams. The world is full of wonder-filled hopes.

I am here to tell you that as far as you're concerned, your days of unfulfilled dreams are over. If you will just open your heart, trust Him, wait for Him, and be willing to go where no man or woman has gone before, everything God has dreamed for you can come to pass.

HE HOLDS HIS DREAM FOR YOU

The heavens are waiting for you to simply say yes. It is amazing but true: God is eager to fulfill the dream He has dreamed for you. He is eager to introduce you to a successfully fulfilling lifestyle. In the pages of this book, you will discover how you can cooperate with God and see everything you've always wanted come to pass.

You will see how this worked in my life. You will see it at work in my wife Cathy's life, and in many, many other people around us. It is often difficult for mere humans to understand that God's focus is completely intent upon His creation and their happiness and sense of fulfillment. He is focused on us. It is true that God is so big He can devote all of His attention to each one of us individually.

CHAPTER 1

Do You Know Who You Are?

As the prophet Mufasa said to his son Simba in the Disney movie classic *The Lion King,* "You are more than you have become." Most of us can say we have heard that from our friends and our family, but few of us understand that God says that to all of us all the time. He made us. Therefore He knows what we are capable of. He knows the power, gifts, and possibilities within that are just waiting to be used. We are more than we have become. There is a deposit within us. Resting within our spirits are inventions, songs, leadership, love, compassion, wisdom, the answers to life's most puzzling questions, and much more. There are depths of comfort, peace, and hope that we cannot imagine. All these things are part of who we are but are largely untapped within. "He is able to do far above what we are able to ask or think" (see Eph. 3:20).

If we can think it, then it is too small. If we can imagine it, God can do far greater. His plan, His dream, His destiny for us is far beyond what our finite minds can comprehend. We see ourselves and our human smallness. We judge ourselves by the mistakes that we make. We determine our probability of success by the failures we have had. We judge our future by our past. We judge what we can do based on what others have told us we cannot do. Our talents are often diminished by the jealous opinions of others. So we live far below who we are. We live far below what we can accomplish.

But you are more than you have become. You already have what you need within you to succeed. You may need education. It might take some training. It might take gaining new experiences. But the raw talent and the gifts that are within you are all you need to become everything God has dreamed for you to become. You, like most people, need to remember who you are. But you may ask, "OK, who am I?" You are a child of God; you are redeemed by the love and sacrifice of Jesus. He loves you. You are the center of His love and attention. He gave Himself completely to you so that you could give yourself completely to Him.

With this as a foundation in your thinking, it becomes easier to see who you really are. For until you know you are accepted, loved, cherished, cared for, and highly favored, it will be difficult for you to understand that He cares enough for you to fulfill every dream, daydream, and desire you have. He holds you in the palm of His hand to cover, protect, and lead you. Because Jesus is in you and you are in Jesus, you can do everything: *"I can do all things through Him who strengthens me"* (Phil. 4:13).

Today can be a new beginning for you. Don't be afraid to trust Him. Don't be afraid to believe Him. He is knocking on the door of your heart. Let Him in then. Give Him room. Watch how the supernatural power of God begins to flow. When the supernatural power of God begins to flow through your life, the supernatural destiny He has for you cannot be far behind.

WHERE DESTINY BEGINS

To say that the supernatural power of God began working in me the first day God called me would be a big mistake. My whole life was preparation for that fateful day when the Lord would show me Himself. The situations and circumstances I have been through, the good times and the bad times, all played a vital role in what was about to unfold for me. But it would be many years before I realized that all of it had a role in preparing me for the supernatural destiny that the Lord dreamed for me before the foundations of the earth.

We often think that we just struggle until God says something to us. We think that until we have a clear call or sense of direction that God isn't paying attention to us, that we are alone. Some think that if we do not keep reminding Him that we are here waiting for Him, we may never hear from Him again. The fact is, He is always speaking to us. He is always leading us. His hand is upon us continuously to take us into the dream He has for us. Most of the time, it is during these times of desperate prayer that we can become aware of what God is already doing. We think that we somehow are convincing Him to love us and that our petitions persuade Him we are worth loving. In reality, our prayer lifts our spiritual awareness so that we begin to see what God has already been doing and what He will do on our behalf: *"For it is God who is at work in you, both to will and to work for His good pleasure"* (Phil. 2:13).

WHEN DESTINY BEGINS

To be perfectly clear, destiny begins before the foundations of the earth, when God dreamed His dreams for you. Then He formed you in your mother's womb with these dreams in mind. God did not leave you out of His plan. He did not forget about you or ignore you. His plans for you are as living and vibrant in His heart as they were when you were a twinkle in His eye!

For many, however, it is difficult to see the work of the Lord in our circumstances. This is especially true when circumstances are difficult and the things we are going through appear to be so far from the destiny we know in our hearts that God has prepared for us. There is no doubt that, without spiritual eyes and the faith that trusts God in every circumstance, trying to respond to the Lord in everyday happenings can, at best be, taxing. The foundation of life is understanding that God loves you and is always dreaming dreams for you, just as loving parents always dream of the best for their children and will do everything they can to see those dreams fulfilled. As God's children, we sometimes do not understand such love and miss an important part of the support mechanism that comes with such love.

We must move beyond the point of just trusting God for our daily needs and supply. We must be able to see Him as the One who not only leads and guides us through the daily circumstances of life, but as the One who has determined that those very circumstances will lead us to the destiny He has prepared. Even the most trying and difficult moments are part of the supernatural lifestyle, for in these moments, God teaches us patience and compassion so that we can go beyond the limitations of ourselves into the things He has for us. These difficulties develop true humility that will cause His presence in our lives to move freely to us and through us. Never underestimate the power of difficult circumstances, for they are the catalysts that will display our humility and softness to the Lord before the nations of the world.

While many people may not initially notice these traits as God-breathed, they will notice them as traits that are pleasing, acceptable, and needful to them. There is no question that softness of heart, gentleness of spirit, and non-prejudicial, unconditional love will open doors for us that no amount of Scripture quoting will ever do. It is far more important to live a Word than to merely quote the Word expecting the people around us to respond. Often, we truly are the only Bible that many people will ever read. We must allow the life of Jesus to shine through us. Then, just as the Scriptures point to Jesus, the life we live will also point to Him. We actually become beacons of hope to those around us. We become living demonstrations of the love, salvation, and healing power of the Lord Jesus whom we serve.

THE DAY THAT CHANGED OUR WORLD

It was not until many months after the initial visitation of the Lord that I realized He had been at work in my life since before I was born.

I do not have time to tell the story in detail in this book, but suffice it to say that God was preparing a way for me for many generations. My grandfather Nori and my grandfather Pasquini came to the United States from Italy at the turn of the 19th century. Both sent for mail-order brides, neither knew English, and neither had a job or a place to live when they arrived. It was their tenacity and desire for a better life that brought them to America. The circumstances that brought my parents together during the Depression is a story all by itself. But once they were married, they immediately were touched with the awful reality of war.

During World War II, my father was drafted into the Army. He reported to a tent, a makeshift military draft office at the Altoona train station, to go for basic training. Having already had his tearful goodbye with my mom, who was then pregnant with my oldest sister, he was faced with the harsh possibility of never seeing her again. But through some incredible circumstances, he was granted a deferment only minutes before he was to board the train that would take him off to war. I cannot even imagine the reunion of my parents just a few hours later. Had he actually gone off to war, I might never have been born.

When Cathy and I were married in January 1973, we could not have been poorer. But as our parents said, "They think they will live on love." The funny thing was, we lived on love in those days, and we continue to live on love. Love for one another, love for others, and of course, the love that bound us together, the love of our Lord Jesus.

CHAPTER 2

The Day Heaven Fell

It was a hot and muggy Friday afternoon. The last thing I wanted to do was drive north on Interstate 81 to make sales calls. As most salesmen know, Friday afternoon cold calling is a difficult task. Folks in general don't like salesmen knocking on their door at any time, but on Friday afternoons, they are particularly unwelcome. But I had a family to feed, bills to pay, dreams to fulfill. Although I didn't particularly like the job I was doing, I loved the fact that during those days of recession and hyper-inflation, the Lord had granted me a job that covered our bills as well as it did. I was reviewing who I would see as I drove north that day when my car was invaded with the Presence of the Lord. You need to understand that I am basically a workaholic. I get focused on a task, and I usually don't put it down until it is done to perfection. So for me to say I was overwhelmed by the Presence of the Lord to the point that I had to pull my car over is quite significant. But that is exactly what happened.

The Presence of the Lord literally invaded my space in the car. One moment I was minding my own business, driving to a potential customer; the next moment I was enraptured by His Presence. The only thing I could do was pull over to the side of the road. It was as though the heavens unzipped over my head. Eternity seemed to drop into my car. It was an amazing experience. All of a sudden nothing else mattered. I was captivated; He had my attention. I did not even have time to be excited about the fact that the Lord was visiting me. I was just consumed by His manifest Presence.

As I peered through this open heaven, the sights and sounds were ones that I will never forget. I was looking into Heaven itself. It is a clamorously joyful dimension! The sounds of worship rang from one side of Heaven to another. Far in the distance was the throne of God. Angels flurried in every direction. I saw what appeared to be messenger angels taking their turn at the throne for a moment or two and then flying off to continue their tasks. Multitudes of people spontaneously fell before the Lord in worship; the sound of their voices shook the foundations of Heaven itself, or so it seemed. The 24 elders worshiped with continuous praise and adoration. There was a deafening, yet wonderful sound in that jubilant atmosphere: Joy, contentment, assurance, security, and peace were the rule of the day. Everywhere I looked, the salvation of the Lord was evident and invigorating.

In this supernatural moment, the next step in God's dream for my family's life was revealed. God's personal intervention changed my life and the life of my family forever. In this atmosphere of His manifest Presence, I wept; I laughed; I raised my hands; I joined in the spontaneous worship of the throngs who worship the Lord continuously before His throne. To say I was caught up in the moment would be an incredible understatement. I did not know God was about to speak to me. To be honest, that never crossed my mind. I was merely joining the power of the moment and the nearness of my Lord. His Spirit touched my spirit; I knew I was His. I knew He loved me. I didn't want to leave. I didn't want anything to change. I have no idea how much time passed as I worshiped and laughed and sang before the Lord.

But at some point, I heard the voice of the Lord: "No one cares about My heart." Those words, to say the least, shocked me. "No one cares what I have to say. My people go about their daily lives unaware that I have much to say, that I have a plan, that I have My own purpose to fulfill in the earth." These words broke my heart, and I responded, "Lord, I care! I care about Your heart! I care about what You have to say! I love Your word; I love to hear Your voice." But the Lord continued to speak as though I had not responded to Him at all: "I have much to say to this generation. I have much for them to do. I am looking for a prophet to publish the prophets."

My response to the Lord was as a willing servant, ignorant as it may have been: "Lord, I will find a prophet for You. I'll help You." My mind began to race. *How do you publish the prophets? How do you get people to read what they have to say? Who are the prophets?* These and many other questions ran through my mind as the Presence of the Lord continued to sweep over me in the car that hot afternoon.

TAKEN!

Immediately I was in a trance. Before I realized what was happening, the Lord and I were standing together in an editor's office. The man sitting at the desk had the traditional old-time editor's visor, and his sleeves were rolled up as he worked on a manuscript. While we stood there watching, an Old Testament prophet came to the door and walked in. He was an interesting sight, to be sure. He wore a typical long robe and had long hair and a beard. (I am sure this was for my benefit. I have always been a little dense.) He was carrying an extremely thick manuscript. He reverently walked over to the editor and laid the manuscript in front of him. The editor did not acknowledge the prophet, never looked up from his work.

He simply took the manuscript and began going through it page by page. He mumbled to himself as he turned the pages: "This won't work!" He crossed out an entire page with his pen, then went to the next page. "No one wants to hear this! You want me to say this?" Then he laughed, crumpled up several more pages, and threw them over his shoulder. The next several minutes were a combination of snide remarks, grumbling, crossing out large amounts of the content, and laughing at the prophet who seemed to have the audacity to think that the editor would really publish what he had said.

To watch the prophet, however, was very interesting. He stood there silently, intermittently shaking his head, with a half smile on his face. It was as though the prophet paid homage to the editor. It was as though he said to the editor, "Do whatever you need to do; just publish the book." I was amazed to see this brief but clear interaction between the prophet of the Lord and the editor who apparently had final control over what ultimately appeared in the book.

It was at this point that I sensed the burning indignation of the Lord. I had no idea what was about to happen. I turned quickly to the Lord, just in time to hear Him say to me, "It is an abomination for My prophets to submit their words to mere mortal men. I am looking for a prophet to publish the prophets." I don't quite understand why, but at that moment, I realized the Lord was talking about me. I had no idea who I was or what I was. I have to admit that at that point I didn't care, as long as I could serve the Lord and be found pleasing to Him.

To this day, I don't care about titles. Titles do not impress me—neither the titles others give, nor the titles some hang so reverently on their chests. I have no concern about what people think of me or how they refer to me. After all these years, my burning, passionate desire is greater than ever.

I only want to be found pleasing in His sight, doing only what He wants me to do. Knowing that my speech, actions, prayers, desires, and work are all done in His Presence keeps me small and soft. It keeps me compassionate and humble. I am painfully aware of who I am and what I am apart from Him. I am painfully aware of my struggles and shortcomings. I am painfully aware of how far I fall short of His glory. I know, beyond a shadow of a doubt, that without Him I am absolutely nothing. I have nothing to brag about. I have nothing I can call my own. For everything I have, everything I am, everything I dream about is because of His unfailing love, His grace, and His never-ending mercy.

On that day I understood, for the first time, the incredible, compassionate, eternal love and mercy that God has for humankind because He has it for me. I am certain that He will do for everyone else what He has done for me. There are few who are less worthy than I am. I know what He has done for me, what He is doing for me, and what He will continue to do for me.

Therefore I am well content with weaknesses, with insults, with distresses, with persecutions, with difficulties, for Christ's sake; for when I am weak, then I am strong (2 Corinthians 12:10).

...I am not ashamed; for I know whom I have believed and I am convinced that He is able to guard what I have entrusted to Him until that day (2 Timothy 1:12).

I have to the best of my ability walked according to the profound awakening of that day. I have walked circumspectly with the deep understanding that all that I have is a gift from God.

WE SAID "YES"

"Lord, I'll do it! Lord, I care about Your word! I want to hear what You have to say. I'll do whatever You want me to do. I'll publish the prophets." At this point, another amazing thing happened. As quickly as the heavens had dropped into the car, the heavens zipped closed. I was alone in the car once again. The change in the spiritual atmosphere was so abrupt that I began to wonder whether I had imagined the entire experience. But tears still streamed from my eyes, His voice still thundered in my spirit, and my heart ached to experience it all again. But the car was empty except for me. I sat there on the side of the road for what seemed to be an hour, but I'm sure was only moments. Once again the heavens unzipped, and all the glory, majesty, joy, and sounds of Heaven dropped into the car. The Lord spoke to me: "If you will treat My word as silver and treat My people as gold, I will cause you to publish the prophets."

Several conflicting emotions swept over me. I felt relieved, excited, frightened, and completely ill-equipped. My university degrees were in elementary education and environmental science. I did not even enjoy reading! At that point in my life, I had no experience, no training, no money, no friends in high places, no idea where to begin. Cathy and I lived in an early nineteenth-century log home with three children. Cathy was pregnant with our fourth son, Joel. Every month we were falling deeper into debt by $100. In 1982 that was a whole lot more than it is today.

There was nothing in our circumstances to confirm that what we had heard was the Lord. From the outside looking in, it was a frivolous attempt to gain attention for ourselves. But contrary to popular teaching, circumstances almost never agree with the word you receive from the Lord. The vision the Lord gave me was easily confirmed by Scripture and by the Presence of the Lord, but ran contrary to everything that could be discerned with the five senses. This resulted in an almost complete rejection of the vision by all those who were our leaders at the time. Only one man, Don Milam, Jr., saw that what we had heard was the Lord. Only he stood with us during the very difficult and tumultuous times that lay ahead. We learned many things over the next several months. We learned who our friends truly were; we experienced the depths of religious jealousy, as well as the inevitability of separation from those who reject the call of God in your life. But we also learned how to stay small as we followed Him. The most difficult lessons were not the lessons of properly handling finances, nor the searching out of authors, nor the logistics of book production or finding markets; the most difficult lessons were the lessons of the heart.

We had to stand as the Lord worked humility, brokenness, and silence deep in our hearts. In the early days, I personally failed at most of these tests of the Lord to burn away ego, anger, and a whole host of other very negative parts of my personality that lay lodged deep in my heart. Little did I know that the building of the man was at least as important as the building of the ministry. Little did I understand that without the brokenness of a man's spirit, his accomplishments would mean little to the generations to come.

Cathy and I discovered that the foundation the Lord was building was, of course, in Him. But we also discovered that the foundation He would build was the foundation of the lives that Cathy and I personally led. The strength of the ministry rested in the strength of our hearts, the brokenness of our spirits, and the genuine dependence we would ultimately have on the Lord. During the difficult years that followed, few people saw the internal workings of the Lord in our hearts as our influence expanded and the effectiveness of "publishing the prophets" moved around the world. Very few people saw the stress that went on in our hearts and in our lives. No one knew of the three mortgages we initially took out on our home. No one knew that we were rejected again and again by banks for a line of credit in order to publish books. No one knew that our company was initially financed with those three mortgages and 20 credit cards.

We dealt with growing criticism from those who believed we had stepped into rebellion by starting a company without the approval of those who supposedly knew better. We struggled with the guilt of uncertainty. We also struggled with the resistance of the marketplace. Most bookstores would not carry charismatic books. Even the Christian Booksellers Association rejected charismatic publishers. We had resistance from without and uncertainty from within our own hearts. Sometimes the pain and confusion was so great we could not find the Presence of the Lord. Sometimes the bills racked up so quickly that we did not know where our next meal was coming from, let alone how we would pay the printing bills.

Are You Kidding Me?

It is funny now to think about, but many people look at us as folks of great faith and power. Many folks see us as unshakable pioneers willing to go to any lengths in order to do the will of God. But the truth was we were frightened little children, constantly concerned that we had stepped out beyond His will, constantly concerned about the welfare of *our* children. We trudged forward, yet deep inside, if we could have, we would have run from it. Yes, you heard me right. The great folks of great faith and power had painted themselves into a corner—we could not run because of the debt we had amassed. Our only hope was to succeed. Although it was difficult—no, impossible—to see at the moment, that in itself was the mercy of God. He knew that we were fundamentally against filing bankruptcy. The Lord knew that our integrity would not allow us to walk away from debt, so He allowed us to get ourselves into a corner where we could not run; therefore, we had to succeed. Many times during this season, I would quietly laugh before the Lord. He had trapped us. He had allowed us into a situation from which there was no escape. Even though we were so desperately frightened, we also knew that it was God's way of preventing us from running from our destiny.

In the early days, our sons didn't understand our circumstances. For instance, at dinnertime Cathy would cook a 3 pound chicken fryer for our family. At that point, our fifth son Stephan had not been born. Cathy would cut up the chicken. Our sons would get the body of the chicken; Cathy would eat the wings; I would get the carcass. The boys were amazed that I always asked for the carcass. They would laugh, not understanding how I could like such a piece of chicken as the carcass. "Oh, dad's eating the carcass again!" I would respond, "I love the carcass! The meat is juicy and sweet! It's the best part of the chicken." I can't tell you the number of times we went through that routine in those early years.

Several years later, when our sons were either in college or married, they often came home for dinner. By this time Cathy was cooking two big roasting chickens for everyone for our dinner. On one particular night, one of my sons was carving the chicken. After the chicken was carved, he brought both carcasses and put them on my plate. He looked at me and smiled: "I guess you still like the carcasses as much as you did when we were kids." He sat down to eat his dinner. I looked at him and said, "Son, I don't need to eat the carcasses anymore." In unison, my sons looked at me with their jaws dropped open. It was the first time they understood why I had only eaten the carcass for those many years. It was an amazing experience for them—very educational, very much a bonding moment.

THE PAIN AND THE POWER

From that point on, everything was…awful! Well, not really everything, but it sure seemed that way. It is unfortunate, but it is true. Most people believe that once they have heard the call of God and are certain of His leading, the rest of the journey will be very easy. But that could not be further from the truth. The stronger the leading of the Lord, the more difficult the journey will certainly be. Very often, the biggest lesson we must learn is humility and brokenness, coming to the realization that the thing that we have been called to do is much, much bigger than we could ever fulfill ourselves. Of course, it takes awhile to understand that. Thus, we enter the process of brokenness. When we are young and excited, ready to serve the Lord in anything, humility and brokenness are far from the center of our attention. Difficulties, over time, bring us to the realization that we are not who we thought we were. This stark realization is one of the most important lessons we will ever learn.

So who are we? We are anointed of God. We are called to serve Him. We are the manifestation of God in the earth. We are lamps for His anointed. We are the light that should not be hidden under a bushel basket. We are the representations of His life and love to the nations. That is why, as I said earlier, our lives are just as important as the ministry we fulfill. How we conduct ourselves in the everyday world is every bit as essential as this thing we are called to do. Some think that because they may be called into business, there is not the scrutiny of lifestyle that there would be had they been called into ministry. But that also is untrue. Our lives are under scrutiny simply because we say we belong to the Lord Jesus. Jesus said, "If the world hates Me, know that it will hate you too. If they persecute Me, they will most certainly persecute you" (see John 15:18). The job description does not enter into play here. It is simply who you are that brings out the good, the bad, and the ugly in all those around us.

But let me say this as well. God does not see us in a different light if we call ourselves ministers or if we are in business. He does not look at us differently if we are homemakers or work in a factory. He sees us all as His sheep; He sees us all as His servants, His friends—those who want union with Him. We are not ranked in importance according to job description or ministry. The believer *is* the priesthood. There is no elitist separation of believers. If we have a pulse, we are in His service. We do not live by faith simply because we depend on the donations of others to live our daily lives. We are not more or less important because we collect an offering or a paycheck. We are all the same. It is a life of faith no matter how we get our income. You are not more spiritual because you wait for the donations of others to take care of your needs. You are not holier than the one who works hard 40, 50, or even 60 hours a week in order to take care of his family. You are not in ministry or out of ministry because of the job you have. God does not separate us by clergy or laity.

We are the priesthood of the believer. We are on a level playing field. He will bless you the same as He will bless me. He will do miracles for the preacher just as quickly as He will do miracles for the homemaker. It is a matter of understanding that that's how God sees us.

When we really understand this, much of our struggle comes to an end. I know who I am. I am in Christ. All the promises that God gave to Abraham, Isaac, and Jacob are mine. All the promises that He has promised any famous pastor, preacher, or evangelist are for you as well. He sees us all as able ministers of the Gospel, carriers of His Presence, carriers of His life and love. Of course, just because we carry His Presence, power, and love, does not mean we must pass out Gospel tracts, pray for everyone we see, or preach the Gospel to everyone on the street. It does mean that we must be willing, able, and open. As the Bible says, we should be ready in season and out of season, when it feels good and when it doesn't feel good. When we sense the Holy Spirit moving in us to do something, we simply respond in the kind, generous, loving way that we understand the Lord Jesus did to all those around Him. He does not bless others because they have a bigger ministry or because their calling is more important than yours.

Here is the good news for you and the bad news for those who want to use you in an unholy, ungodly way. Your life is every bit as important as the most famous believer you know. Your responsibility to your world is as critical as a famous person's responsibility is to his or her world. How often do we get depressed when we hear someone talking about his or her call to change the world? How often does that just make us want to give up, to decide we can never be as effective as others? Well, I have more good news. We are called to change the world. But the world we change is our world. We are responsible for those we touch on a daily, weekly, monthly basis. Our world is that sphere of influence, that circle of friends that we personally interact with regularly. For some folks, their influence may be their neighborhood. For others, their sphere of influence may be their community. For others still, it may be the Church, the nation, or the world. But the most important thing for us to understand is that we are responsible for whatever our world happens to be. This makes our calling a lot more realistic, a lot more tangible, and a lot more certain to be adequately fulfilled.

CHAPTER 3

The True Cutting Edge

How many times have you heard someone say, "How would you like to be on the cutting edge of God's work?" How many of you dream of the day that your daily life can be fulfilled by doing things that are exactly on the cutting edge of God's desired activity in the earth? It is amazing how much of what we hear tends to separate us from union with the Lord. It can put us at a distance from the will of God, just beyond the reach of destiny. It can keep us just beyond the security of really knowing that we are doing something significant for the Lord. That is because most ministries want you to join them in prayer support, volunteer support, and most importantly, financial support.

If these organizations can get you to feel less than fulfilled, then they have control of you.

Let me pause here to say something very important. I am not talking about those organizations that simply ask you for your support. Organizations like Samaritan's Purse, Compassion International, and many others are valid mission organizations. These selfless, God-serving organizations simply tug on your heartstrings to help those who are in need. Many billions of dollars are given every year to these worthwhile causes. But these are not the causes to which I refer. I refer to those organizations that make you feel unfulfilled, doing much less than you should for the Lord in order to please Him.

These organizations tout themselves as so Christ-centered, so prophetic in nature that they are literally on the cutting edge of God's prophetic activity. These organizations will proclaim that your participation with them financially will put you also on the cutting edge of God's activity. They will tell you that it is too bad that you are in a situation where you can't do anything for God, but if you give money to them, then your life will be worth living. Your donations, your prayers, and your service all come together to make your life seem fulfilled as you live on the cutting edge of somebody else's dream.

I know this sounds difficult. But there is freedom in what I am about to say. If you listen, you'll hear destiny opening its doors to you. The cutting edge of God is not what famous ministries are doing. If you personally, in your home, in your work, and in your neighborhood are doing what God is telling you to do, then you are on the cutting edge of His activity. That cutting-edge activity cannot be defined by someone else. God's prophetic edge can only be defined in your own heart according to what He is speaking to you.

For instance, I know a woman who is a greeter at a Wal-mart. God told her to take that job. She goes to work every day knowing she is entering her mission field. She can't say "God bless you" to everyone. She can't pray for people. She can't pass out Scripture verses. But she understands the power of impartation. She understands her smile, her greeting, and even an occasional handshake transmits the Presence and the power of God to those who pass by, whether or not they are born again. This woman understands she is carrying the very Presence of God within her, and she allows that Presence to flow through her in whatever she is doing.

There are many people in many walks of life who simply go about doing the will of their Father in Heaven. They do not allow themselves to be intimidated or discouraged by those who would demand loyalty to their organization for their financial or spiritual well-being. Taking responsibility for your neighborhood does not require Gospel tracts, a Bible study, a weekly song service, or bumper stickers all over your car. Changing your world simply means doing whatever God wants you to do. I have often heard people say that although they continually pray to be used by God, they don't hear Him telling them to do anything. I ask them, "So, what do you do?" The answers I get vary, but most of the answers indicate that they are already doing what they are waiting to hear God tell them to do. Just being a good neighbor is a great expression of God's life and love. Being a kind and concerned co-worker or an encourager of your family is an excellent planting of God's glory and yields much fruit.

You may think, *What does this have to do with supernatural destiny?* And that would be a good question. But supernatural destiny begins exactly where you are. Destiny begins with an open heart and open spirit. Whatever your hand finds to do, do it with all your heart (see Eccles. 9:10; Col. 3:23; 1 Sam. 10:7). If your heart is not open to the little things that only He sees, what makes you think you will be open to the dreams He has for you? These are proving grounds. These are days of preparation, training, and discernment. Don't let them slip through your fingers. They are essential to your future.

> *Whatever you do, do your work heartily, as for the Lord rather than for men, knowing that from the Lord you will receive the reward of the inheritance. It is the Lord Christ whom you serve* (Colossians 3:23-24).

He watches us, and as He sees us faithful with the little things, He blesses us with the greatest things. While others may not see what you do, God sees. While others may not understand your motivation, you know you are under orders from a higher plane of existence. You march to a drummer from another dimension. The most exciting life of destiny begins with quietly and wholeheartedly blessing, praying, and doing whatever your hand finds to do. This silent, hidden work that you do unto the Lord yields a future that you cannot imagine. My challenge to you is to understand who you are. You are His. You carry His Presence, His power, His life. Whatever you do, do it unto the Lord. Destiny begins the first time you say "yes" to Him and grows over a lifetime of personal obedience.

When I was a student at a local university, I led a weekly student prayer and praise service with hundreds of students. I also had a job as a janitor at the university café, which was always crowded and always a mess. My last responsibility at the end of the workday was to clean the bathrooms. So every Thursday night at 6 P.M. I was on my knees scrubbing out the toilets and wiping messes off the floor. At 6:30 P.M. I was on my knees in prayer as the service began. No one knew my job description until the telltale smell of Pine-Sol wafted over the students. The Lord could trust me to clean the bathrooms and then could also trust me to clean hearts. It was a hard, but ultimately, a very rewarding lesson!

CHAPTER 4

Always
Small Beginnings

I had discovered the perfect place to grow in Christ, who is, after all, our ultimate destiny. That perfect place was over those toilets! Whatever your hand finds to do, do with all your heart (see Eccles. 9:10; Col. 3:23). We sometimes forget that God is training us from the moment we are born. But too often, it takes us a long time to realize we are being trained. Some people never discover that. They go through life with no apparent destination, no apparent purpose, and certainly no apparent understanding that God has dreams kept for them in His heart.

For it is just like a man about to go on a journey, who called his own slaves, and entrusted his possessions to them. To one he gave five talents, to another, two, and to another, one, each according to his own ability; and he went on his journey. Immediately the one who had received the five talents went and traded with them, and gained five more talents. In the same manner the one who had received the two talents gained two more. But he who received the one talent went away and dug a hole in the ground and hid his master's money. Now after a long time the master of those slaves came and settled accounts with them. The one who had received the five talents came up and brought five more talents, saying, "Master, you entrusted five talents to me. See, I have gained five more talents." His master said to him, "Well done, good and faithful slave. You were faithful with a few things, I will put you in charge of many things; enter into the joy of your master." Also the one who had received the two talents came up and said, "Master, you entrusted two talents to me. See, I have gained two more talents." His master said to him, "Well done, good and faithful slave. You were faithful with a few things, I will put you in charge of many things; enter into the joy of your master." And the one also who had received the one talent came up and said, "Master, I knew you to be a hard man, reaping where you did not sow, and gathering where you scattered no seed. And I was afraid, and went away and hid your talent in the ground. See, you have what

*is yours." But his master answered and said to him,
"You wicked, lazy slave, you knew that I reap where I
did not sow and gather where I scattered no seed. Then
you ought to have put my money in the bank, and on
my arrival I would have received my money back with
interest"* (Matthew 25:14-27).

Little did these servants realize that their future wisdom depended upon what they did now with their lives. The young rarely understand that we build on current success. Success is one right decision after another. It is not predestined. Success is no accident. Success is the by-product of a series of right decisions.

Everything matters. Everything. Life matters. We are not players in the football game where most of the team stands on the sidelines waiting to be called into the game. We are all in the game. Every decision we make, every word we say, paves a road upon which we must travel. Many erroneously believe that God only begins to speak to us or work with us once we have discovered why we were born. But, as I have tried to point out thus far, nothing could be further from the truth. Your daily activities are essential to your future. What we do now, what we think now, and what we participate in now forms our personality, our spirit, and ultimately our future.

Expecting to fulfill our destiny without preparation is like an Olympian expecting to win the gold medal without having prepared herself for the event in which she is competing. I have been walking with the Lord for 40 years. I have done many things, accomplished many exciting goals. But everything I have done has been a preparation for the road I must now travel. Do not make the mistake of thinking that God is not involved with you simply because you are not certain of the destiny He has for you.

I slowly began to understand how everything prepares me for my destiny. I was able to look back in my life and see events that undoubtedly prepared me. Many times over these years as a publisher, I have seen how all the extremely difficult, painful, and even heartbreaking events of my life made me into the man I needed to be in order to walk the road laid before me with integrity, circumspection, and peace.

Yes, everything matters. Everything I do has an impact on my soul. Everything I do shapes my future and forms the opinions and attitudes that will guide me through the rest of my life. It was an amazing discovery for me. Even before I knew God wanted me to publish books, He was preparing me to publish books. There were times that I felt utterly alone, even forgot that God had called me. But He never forgot. Even when I did not sense His nearness, He was at work to bring about His perfect pleasure in my life. He was at work to mold me into the kind of person that He could use. That's why I can say with so much confidence—whatever I am, I am by the grace of God. Whatever I have accomplished, I accomplished because of His life and love to me, in me, and through me. I owe everything I am to Him. I may not be everything I should be. Many flaws still are glaring and embarrassing, but whatever good I have accomplished was because of Him alone.

Had that last servant understood the consequences, he most certainly would have worked harder to turn profit for his master. He had no idea what the master was doing; therefore, he could not and did not respond properly. We must understand that the master is constantly handing talents to us. Whether we know it or not, He hands them to us. He gives us talents with which He will determine our readiness to do His will. Make no mistake; He is a sovereign God, but He does not violate the will of human beings. He does not violate that sacred ability that we have to make our own decisions and formulate our futures.

My challenge to you right now is for you to begin to see with spiritual eyes. Acknowledge that He is at work in you to work out His pleasure for you. He has a plan for you. He has dreamed a dream for you. In fact, He has dreamed many dreams for you, and His anticipation is to lead and guide you. In my experience, the fullness of joy is living out all the dreams that He has dreamed for you. That process began before the foundations of the earth. He knew you, as the psalmist said, when He formed you in your mother's womb (see Ps. 139). He formed you with your destiny in mind. He formed you with the dreams that He has dreamed for you in the forefront of His thoughts. He is intimately, wholeheartedly, completely, and single-mindedly at work with you, in you, and through you to bring about all that He has planned for you.

GOD ALWAYS CONFIRMS HIS CALLING

I will not leave you as orphans; I will come to you
(John 14:18).

There is one thing for certain: God always helps us along the journey in ways we could never imagine. I always enjoyed it when God gave us signs to help us recognize the calling that was on our lives. I enjoyed them because I really needed them to build and reassure my faith! It was amazing that these times would always come during the most difficult circumstances. He knew what we struggled with. He knew the strength we needed just to put one foot in front of the other. There were times when Cathy and I were not sure of very much beyond God's love for us and our love for each other.

I wish I could say we were always the great people of faith and power that so many believe we were; the truth is, we struggled a lot. But God is faithful all the time. He was there to encourage us on even in the most difficult circumstances. I must admit that sometimes the situation seemed so bleak that we were unable to hear the word of the Lord to encourage us. During those times we had to go back to the initial call. We had to remember the four-day vision that God had given me. I had to review what occurred during the four days of being in a trance and seeing God's desire for us. *"In that day you will know that I am in My Father, and you in Me, and I in you"* (John 14:20).

There was the time when God gave us an incredible signal that we were definitely on the path that He had called us to. Early one morning I sat in my office, praying for God's wisdom and for what I was to do that day. It was a difficult morning; the bills were piling up, and fear controlled me to the point where I was almost frozen, unsure of what to do next. But as I began to go about my daily to-do list, I heard the voice of the Lord speaking very clearly to me: "I want you to call _____ [a certain charismatic leader]." I knew this charismatic leader by reputation very well. He was one of the most popular prophetic leaders in the '70s and early '80s. God spoke to me: "This man is waiting for your phone call. I need you to take over his publishing. He is being abused by his current publisher, and his royalty is not being paid." *Could this be the Lord?* I thought to myself. *Is this something God is saying to me?* But I didn't have to ask that too many times, for I was certain I had heard the Lord.

You can't imagine how frightened I was to call this man, being so new in book publishing. I had no reason to believe he would trust me. I was certain he would have no idea who I was. Rather than making the direct call as I was instructed, I called a mutual friend who knew this man personally. My friend called this charismatic prophetic leader only to hear a remarkable story on the other side. This gentle prophet told my friend, "The Lord woke me at 4 A.M. this morning to tell me I was being cheated by my publisher and that I needed to get out. The Lord told me not to worry though; He would speak to another publisher, and that publishing company would call me the same day." As amazing as that sounds, my friend had called within three hours of the time the Lord spoke to me on that same morning. It was a set of circumstances made in Heaven. It was a clear and powerful confirmation that we were hearing the Lord and that He was leading our every step. It brought back to mind something the Lord spoke to me before we started the company: "If you treat My word as silver and My people as gold, I will cause you to publish the prophets." The Lord showed me that He would be my marketing department; He would draw men and women to us so that we would not need to spend a lot of time and money searching out new authors. The ones who heard were the ones we were to publish.

Now I wish this individual story had a happy ending. It does, and it doesn't. It does have a happy ending because it confirmed God's call on our lives. It doesn't have a happy ending because I was so unsure of myself that I turned the negotiations over to another publisher who quickly and decidedly signed that author to a contract under his own label, completely leaving me out of the picture. To this day, that event stands as a monument to my weakness and to God's faithfulness, as well as a poignant reminder of the discernment that is necessary when deciding who to trust and who not to trust—even in Christian publishing. I also decided that it was not in the best interests of this dear prophetic man to be embroiled in the truly dark side of "Christian" publishing. May God cause righteous men and women to arise in all areas of Christian business and ministry.

This was just one more time when Cathy and I had to learn to leave the past in the hands of the Lord, to leave our mistakes at the Cross, and to find a place of personal repentance and move forward. After all, I was the one who decided to bring others into something the Lord had clearly instructed me to do. My lack of self-confidence cost me dearly and opened the door to those of little integrity. Cathy had wisely counseled me for many years that my greatest strength is also my greatest weakness. With this event, I finally understood. I have a very strong pastor's heart. That pastor's heart wants to always think the very best of everyone, hope the best for everyone, make every opportunity for everyone. If there's one thing we must learn early in our lives, it is that even our gifts must be under the Lordship of Jesus. Our gifts must be under the leading of God, or those gifts will destroy us.

Let me give you an example. Cathy and I are both avid givers. Some people would say chronic givers; others would say it is an addiction. (I can think of worse things to be addicted to!) The point is that we have discovered that it is much, much better to give than it is to receive. But that gift of giving needs to be under the Lordship of Jesus. More than once, our giving nearly caused us to go bankrupt. The only way we can be givers our entire lives is to allow our giving to be under His Lordship. If we go bankrupt, our giving ends, but if we allow God to direct our giving, we can give forever. That means we are not moved by the stories of either foreign missions, famous televangelists, or local youth groups taking trips overseas. Emotional giving accounts for much of the giving in America. It is good to be compassionate, but we must be led by the Spirit, not by our emotions. Our giving must be under the Lordship of Jesus. We must give only to those we are sure we are to give to and then give only what the Lord wants us to give.

Some believers have determined that it is truly spiritual to burn yourself out for the Lord. Some believe that giving to the point of poverty is holy. Still others believe that ministry that costs you your family is a deep commitment which God ordains. These are not pious actions. They are simply religious and, hence, stupid. When we give, serve, minister by the Holy Spirit, He always refreshes, rebuilds, and resupplies. When we go in our own strength, the result is devastation.

Nonetheless, at this very difficult time in the early days of our ministry, God confirmed deep in our hearts that His hand was upon us. He had paid us the greatest of all compliments. He told an author that He would send him someone that he could trust. Of all the accolades one could receive in this world, this confirmation from the Lord stands head and shoulders above anything a mere man could say to support my ministry, my call, or my life. When you spend your life seeking His glory and working under His hand, you will live your life being able to change the world in ways you could not have possibly imagined. At the end of the day, it is not the recommendation of man that we need; it is the confirmation of the Spirit of God that actually opens the windows of Heaven and the doors of favor. When man ordains man, he gets the title of bishop, apostle, pastor, prophet, etc. But when God calls you, you get the title, "friend of God."

MIRACLES HAPPEN

There was another extremely difficult time financially when we saw God's hand break through. It was probably the last place we ever expected a miracle to come from—Hawaii—but on this particular day, we would have taken a miracle from the moon!

I had just received a call from our printer. The collection department carried the bad news: Unless we made a payment of $5,000 within 24 hours, they would freeze the several books that were ready to be produced. I had promised authors books by a specific date. I had set up books to be received by bookstores by a specific date. I was expecting payment from stores and distributors that had not come in. But, as I am sure you know, bill collectors don't want excuses. They want better planning on our part. They were right. But I also could not afford to have the presses turned off either.

What made this crisis particularly unusual was the enemy's attempt to get me to do something unethical. I had been approached by a specific author with a book that he wanted published. As I read through the manuscript, it was clear that this was not a book that I wanted to publish. There were many things that made me uncomfortable, not the least of which was that it had a bad spirit about it. I could not bring myself to approve this book, even though publishing the book would provide exactly the amount of money I needed to make payment to the printing company. We are not a vanity press or a self-publishing company. We do, however, require specific pre-purchase of books to be certain that the author will work as hard as we do to get the book into the market. We have discovered that, in this publishing niche called charismatic books, the author's endorsement and presentation of the product seems to be the most important aspect of the entire marketing program.

This author was ready and willing to purchase the books required ($3,000). Unfortunately, I could not get the release of the Holy Spirit to publish the book. I informed the author that I was not going to work with him. I said goodbye to him, and he left the office. Early the next morning, I had barely finished my first cup of coffee when this author appeared at the front desk. He was taken back to my office where he again pitched the need for us to publish this book for him. "I can sense you are in need," this author began, "so I want to give you a personal gift. This gift is not toward the purchase of the books I need. It is simply a gift to tell you that I appreciate your hard work and your sensitivity to the Holy Spirit. It is a gift so that you know I believe in you. I have made this check out to you personally so that you can spend it solely on the needs of your family. And then we can talk about publishing my book."

I wish I could say that I rose up in the strength and power of the living God, but I didn't. The bad news, at this point, is that I succumbed to the temptation. I took the check. He walked out of the building a happy man. But it didn't take too many hours before I began to feel the deep conviction of the Holy Spirit. I knew the Lord did not want me to publish the book. Before I had an opportunity to convince myself that it was OK to proceed, I took the check and tore it into a thousand tiny pieces. Then I called the author and told him the deal was off and that I had destroyed the check.

One series of troubles may have ended, but another problem still existed. I had less than 24 hours to get a check for $5,000 to the printer. I went to bed that night wondering if the next day would be the last day of Destiny Image Publishers.

In spite of the miracles that kept us going, in spite of the four-day vision I had, my faith was shaken that day. I felt that I had barely won a battle, but I wondered if I had lost the war.

As I lay there in bed, my mind went back to a meeting I had with another very popular charismatic writer of that time. He had published dozens of books and hundreds of magazine articles. I believed that if anyone would confirm my visions, he would. Much to my shock, he agreed to meet with me. In our meeting, I carefully laid out the visions I had and explained God's instruction to me concerning the publishing industry and my calling to publish and care for prophetic voices. He gave me one of the most devastating responses I had received to that point. As I finished my presentation, he said without hesitation, "I am sure you have heard from the Lord. The need for such a publishing company is great, but I am afraid you will not be able to do it. I suspect that in a few months, we will find your battered and bloody body along the roadside of God's will along with all the others who have tried to do the same thing." *OK, then*, I thought to myself, *no help here.* The meeting ended abruptly but graciously. Cathy and I made the long drive home in silence. It was so difficult. For all the respected men who told us we were wrong, we could not shake the sense within that He wanted us to go on. That meeting was "the last nail in the coffin," as it were. Our reputation, such as it was, was absolutely gone. We were tagged, marked, excluded. But we had heard from God.

This night, with the unpaid bill looming over us, I again began to search my heart, my attitude, and my feelings. I drifted off to sleep with no resolution.

The next morning I headed into the office. The Federal Express truck was parked in front of the building, as it often was, delivering manuscripts or edits to the office from the editors we were using from around the country. But this morning was different, for there came by Federal Express an overnight letter that was obviously not thick enough to have a manuscript. In fact, it was so light that I wondered if there was anything in it at all. But, to my surprise, this envelope contained yet another major confirmation that God indeed had called us and was working out the details. In this envelope was a check for $5,000. It came from a man who wrote a letter that had been dated three days earlier. The letter stated that the Lord had instructed him to write me a check and overnight it immediately. Back in those days, overnight from Hawaii meant three days.

It is amazing how the Lord works according to what He knows we will do—for this check was written and sent three days before I needed it. It was sent before I had erroneously taken the check from that author and before I decided not to keep the check. I didn't know, but God knew. He had this fine man, obedient to the Lord, respond to my need. He was not a rich man. He was an insurance man, a hard-working American Christian, just like most of us. But this day he heard the word of the Lord. This day God used him to confirm to me and my wife Cathy, once again, that we were in the center of His will and purposes. Whatever Destiny Image accomplishes in the years to come, it is certain that this man's reward will contain part of the success of what we have done. His selfless faithfulness is a testimony that Christ should have the freedom to use us however He sees fit. This act was a tremendous lesson to Cathy and me. Although we had been givers for many years, we once again saw how the purposes of God are fulfilled by average people who simply know the voice of the Lord and are obedient to Him.

CHAPTER 5

The Holy Spirit Corrects the Course

Your word is a lamp to my feet and a light to my path (Psalm 119:105).

Walking out God's plan for your life is much like following a GPS on a road trip. Although you have only one destination, there are many turns during the journey. Visionaries often respond to the initial word of the Lord to step out and begin to experience their supernatural destiny, but fail to be open to the fact that they are on a journey. The destination is the same, but the road to that destination will change many times. In the early days of Destiny Image, our family traveled to many conferences together. We visited many authors and publishers as a family. Back in those days we had a conversion van we took everywhere, putting hundreds of thousands of miles on the road.

But for every one of those miles we traveled, we had to be constantly looking at the map. We understood that to get to our final destination we were not going to stay on one road for very long. But that did not mean that the road we had been traveling on was incorrect. Sometimes, it was time to turn in order to arrive at the final destination. It was not hard to understand that one road simply led to the next. If we were unwilling to make the turns that our map told us to make, we would never get to where we needed to be. A journey, by definition, suggests necessary attention to the world around you to be certain you stay the correct course. One correct turn did not guarantee that the next turn would be reached. It required eternal diligence to finish the journey.

Whether it is pleasant or unpleasant, we will listen to the voice of the Lord our God to whom we are sending you, so that it may go well with us when we listen to the voice of the Lord our God (Jeremiah 42:6).

Our calling is no different. One direction shift does not guarantee, or even indicate, that it is the last one. Being led by the Spirit and giving discernment preeminence is the key to continued success.

Once again, discernment becomes a major factor in our life's journey. The God who launched us on our supernatural journey is the same God who leads us to change course when the time comes. To say that another way, our grand adventure called life is made up of many, many smaller adventures. They can all be exciting; they're all our Lord; they all teach us the ways of the Lord. But the end of one small journey marks the beginning of the next; thus, our grand journey continues through time.

Without sounding contradictory, I also need to speak to the other side of this issue. Sometimes a side venture becomes so exciting that we don't want to finish the journey. The key issue is to be able to discern the leading of the Lord. We do not serve a random God. Guidance is not a game. Our Lord never plays cat and mouse. There is far too much to be accomplished. He wants us to learn our lessons so that we can go on the journey He has for us. Again I must talk about discernment; the leading of the Lord is paramount in all we do. We must be careful that our own personal desires and need for success do not govern the voice of the Lord. It is far easier to respond to our own personal desires than it is to hear the voice of the Lord to change direction or to move on from where we have camped. To keep our supernatural destiny fresh, vibrant, relevant, and successful, we must stay in touch with the Spirit of the Lord. We must know what He is calling us to do and be willing to let Him adjust us at any point. *"He leads the humble in justice, and He teaches the humble His way"* (Ps. 25:9).

Sometimes our humility can be tested, and we can be taught by those we least expect to hear from. Such was the case on a trip to Orlando, Florida. My middle son, Matthew, then seven years old, attended the conference with me. I always took at least one of my sons with me everywhere I went. This helped remind me of one of the most important reasons I was doing what I was doing, as well as gave me family companionship. I am a real softy at heart. I can't be away from the family for too long!

We arrived at the Orlando Marriott to discover that many of the vendors had already arrived. All of us knew that the placement of your table was directly related to the number of sales you would get. Placement close to the main entrance was sure to guarantee a good conference. Being at the end of the hallway or even in another corridor, however, greatly limited the possibility of a good event. When you are in any business, you learn quickly and sometimes painfully that trusting God does not negate the need for good common sense that results in sales. I have graciously learned that God covers our ignorance, but He eventually expects us to learn the secrets of whatever trade we are in. Bills cannot be paid with a Bible verse, nor are salaries paid with a smile and a promise. The cold, hard facts of life are simple. Cash keeps the ministries flowing. The cash either comes from sales or donations, but it's the cash, no matter where it comes from, that produces progress in the ministry.

Matthew and I arrived at the vendor registration area. We greeted several of the other businesses and ministries who were there to set up a booth. When the conference director entered, everyone pushed their way to him, wanting to be the first to be assigned the place nearest to the worship conference entrance. Unfortunately, I must admit that I was caught up in the frenzy of the moment. I am embarrassed to tell you that I became angry that I had traveled more miles than anyone there, and would probably end up with the worst spot. My son Matthew, although very young, could tell I was unhappy about the situation. He took me by the hand and pulled me away from the crowd. With his big, reassuring smile, he said to me, "Dad, it's OK. Jesus knows what we need." I stared into his little face, and I melted with embarrassed repentance.

Instead of joining in the fray for position, we walked to the ice cream shop on the far side of the hotel. There we each had a double chocolate ice cream cone and a Pepsi. A half hour later we walked back to the vendor registration table. The coordinator was there alone. My heart sank. I had blown it. He was done assigning spaces. But he looked at me and smiled, "Oh, there you are! I thought I saw you before; then you disappeared. I have your display space assigned." I looked at him and smiled, knowing that I was probably back in the corner somewhere. Much to my shock, he had given us the primary place at the entrance of the main events. "I put you here," he said, "because you always have good lighting and the biggest displays—and because you came farther than anybody else." I looked at him with a grateful heart, and then I looked to Matthew who beamed from ear to ear. "I knew Jesus would take care of us," was all he said to me. *"A man's pride will bring him low, but a humble spirit will obtain honor"* (Prov. 29:23).

Our willingness to be able to hear the voice of the Lord through anyone at any time is a great advantage. Allowing ourselves to be corrected by our children, no matter how young they are, is a great advantage to the work of the ministry. I learned many years ago that surrounding myself with "yes-men" was probably the most dangerous thing I could do. Men and women who think for themselves offer the greatest opportunity for balance, growth, and ultimately success. Balance is never in the man, but in the Body. Opening my heart and life to those other vantage points and ministries helps to keep me spot on. When I am too big to be corrected, I am finished as far as my effectiveness is concerned.

There is a difference between self-thinking and self-promoting. Self-thinkers will hear what you have to say. They will respectfully and humbly analyze your decision. Often they will think of other alternatives, some of which may be superior to the decision you made. Listening to these folks has protected me many times over the years. They have prevented me from making mistakes that I would most certainly regret and that would have cost me a lot of money. The times I ignored their counsel I have often regretted it.

Self-promoters, conversely, are those who will take your decision and try to adjust it based on what is best for them. They will try to improve your answer for the sake of showing you up or because they are vying for a better position. But, at the end of the day, the work is not about them, even as it is not about you. The work is always about the Lord Jesus. It is always about His calling, His destiny for you, and the plan He has laid out so you could succeed in that destiny. These self-promoters are dangerous at best. God give us true discernment to be able to see these folks before they do irreparable harm to the work of the Lord.

SIDESHOWS NOT ALLOWED!

One adventure sticks out as a very strong lesson to us. One of our favorite journeys was to Atlanta, Georgia. Many booksellers' conventions, pastors, and authors seem to be located in and around the Atlanta area, so we often drove in that direction. In the last stretch of highway between Charlotte, North Carolina, and Atlanta, Georgia, there is a rest area designed specifically for kids. There is a small-town water tower shaped and painted like a peach, which is, of course, Georgia's state fruit. Our sons loved that rest stop. There were playgrounds, vending machines, and grass to have a picnic. It would have been easy to spend hours there. In fact, it was always difficult to get our sons back into the van when it was time to continue the journey. They often cried that they wanted to just stay there at the rest stop rather than go on to the destination. They did not understand that, as exciting as the rest stop was, the destination would not only be better, but was in fact, the reason for the journey. How many times do we get sidetracked on our journey? How many times is the road so good that we don't want to go on? Hmm, that happened to the children of Israel when many of the tribes decided to camp on the wrong side of the Jordan River.

The most incredible thing I discovered on my journey was that God, who called me, had every intention of bringing to the fulfillment all He showed me He would do. He didn't start me on this journey just to leave me alone to fail. Success was and is as much a part of the plan as the original vision I saw in 1982.

> *Moreover, the Lord showed great and distressing signs and wonders before our eyes against Egypt, Pharaoh and all his household; He brought us out from there in order to bring us in, to give us the land which He had sworn to our fathers* (Deuteronomy 6:22-23).

WHAT HAS THE POWER?

This self-evaluating question is most important. What has the power over our lives? What is the final authority on what we will do? Sometimes our past has the power; sometimes our history rules our future. What have we done in the past that was very successful? Many times, we think that future success is completely dependent upon rediscovering and redoing what we've done in the past. Nothing could be further from the truth. His mercies are new every morning; His faithfulness is great (see Lam. 3:23). Yesterday is gone; tomorrow has not yet arrived; there is only success and happiness in today. But if we can only judge today by what felt good yesterday, then we will miss the real joys and pleasures of living in the present.

In the early days of Destiny Image, my problem was looking too intently into the future to find peace. I was convinced that I simply had to endure today, and then someday I would have success. The joy was not in today; the joy was in tomorrow. Of course, as we all know, tomorrow never comes; therefore, the joy never comes. Unfortunately, that attitude caused me to miss a lot of the present, a lot of good times I could have had with Cathy and my children. I was too engulfed in my own calling to understand the needs of Cathy and the family.

Thank God she is such a good woman. She carries the fires of His purposes as intensely as I do, so she understood what I faced. But my life was a life of struggle, yearning, and uncertainty. My family wondered whether or not I enjoyed being with them, whether I even loved them. Of course I loved them, but my actions showed them otherwise. It took years and lots of personal heartache to get that through to my heart. Thank God for His patience—and thanks to my family for their patience as well! *"...today if you hear His voice, do not harden your hearts, as when they provoked Me"* (Heb. 3:15).

HE WILL ALWAYS TEACH US

Vacation sounds like a strange time to learn a lesson, but in my experience, He never misses a moment to teach me something. Early one August morning, we awoke to begin packing for our yearly trip to the beach. To be honest, nobody looked forward to our preparation day. Dad (me) was hard to get along with. Then, after we arrived at the beach, it was like Dad threw a switch, and the week was fun. But on this particular morning, God spoke to me before my feet hit the ground. "Don, today your vacation starts right now." I didn't think too much of it at the time, so I jumped up out of bed and began to send orders from one side of the house to the other. But the voice of the Lord came to me again, "Don, your vacation begins right now." I can't honestly tell you at what point I got it, but sometime during that day I did. And although it took time, it began to change how I thought about vacation, and, more importantly, life in general.

"Vacation starts today," the Lord said very clearly to me. But it sank into my spirit at a much deeper level. The phrase, "life starts today," made its way deep into my spirit. The happiness, joy, peace, relaxation, and fun that we all enjoyed at the beach were the same attitudes we should be enjoying together all the time, whether we are packing the car, driving to the beach, or sitting on the beach. "Life begins today." I had always imagined that success would be a point in time with the same kind of transition from drudgery to fun as the shift between driving to the beach and arriving there. I was certain it was a point in time. We would arrive at the beach. As soon as the car doors opened, attitudes would change. We had arrived! The struggle was over; it was time to have fun! Unfortunately, life isn't that way.

Joy, peace, love, and patience are all things that we only have right now. There is no tomorrow. Success in life doesn't come as a point in time in which one minute you don't have success, and the next minute you do. Success is an attitude. Victory is an attitude. Hope is an attitude. These attitudes and many more come with the understanding that you live with the gifts God gave you now. Since success is an attitude, it's not a switch that can be turned on and off. The world judges success by income, the extent of your calling, and the number of Facebook friends/fans you have. But in Christ, success is completely different. He is the one who rewards love, peace, patience, honor, respect, and faith. These attitudes release the power of faith in your life. These attitudes have power we do not understand. No wonder the Scripture says, referring to man, *"For as he thinks within himself, so he is"* (Prov. 23:7).

When I understood what true success was, I realized that life was to be lived now and not in the future. That thought changed my attitude about everything. I had been a Christian for forty years, and I had major misunderstandings of how I was to live life and show love to my wife and family. *"For what shall it profit a man, if he shall gain the whole world, and lose his own soul?"* (Mark 8:36 KJV). That question can be just as validly asked this way, "What does it profit a man if he gains great recognition and success, but loses his own family?"

PAINFUL DECISIONS

"How can I lay off a friend? I just can't walk in there tomorrow and tell these people that I have known and loved for so long that I can no longer give them work." I wrestled in prayer late into the night. I did not like what I was hearing the Holy Spirit telling me to do. It was not as though I didn't understand our situation. The Brownsville Revival and Toronto Blessing were winding down. We had published many books during those two extraordinary seasons. The books we published helped document as well as spread the hope of God's manifest Presence worldwide. We had hired many people to take care of the increased workload as we published and distributed book after book.

But these two spectacular moments in history were passing away. Hank Hanegraaff, a self-appointed, West Coast guardian of all things Christian, had rejected these moves as demonically inspired. Again, this appalling lack of discernment both in him and in the Body of Christ in general had robbed the world of the best opportunity for the permanent restoration of His manifest Presence that we had seen in nearly 100 years.

The day Hanegraaff first went on his nationally syndicated radio show with his rash judgments, unscriptural interpretations, and personal accusations of demonic influence, the religious public became too frightened to continue participating in these movements. Believers all over the country were confused and frightened. This man required a scriptural veracity that he did not apply to himself, else he would have pleaded with these men privately as the Scriptures demand when situations like this occur in the Body of Christ. His radio certainly scattered the sheep. Book sales came to an end almost overnight. We had to act, and we had to act fast. We were not like the local church system that would just keep going and take more offerings. Like any other business, we had to live within our means. We had to creatively discover new ways to proclaim the word of the Lord. We had to find new ways to stay within our budget when these sales waned.

So this night I was wrestling with the Lord, not wanting to make the decisions I needed to make, not wanting to face these people who believed in me and in the vision God gave to us.

Once again, our Lord came through. As I prayed, I fell into a trance, and the Lord gave me a vision that would forever alter my view of Christian ministry. In this dream, I was the fire chief. I sat in the front of the big fire truck followed by a whole team of vehicles. We were headed for a mountain that was threatened by forest fire. Bells rang, whistles blew, lights flashed. We were on our way to save the day. As we reached the foot of the mountain, my eyes fell upon a huge pine tree. It was magnificent in every way; the tree seemed to go on forever into the sky. But it had just started to burn. I immediately ordered the team off the road. We circled the tree, pulled out every firefighting apparatus we had, and focused our attention on that tree. It didn't take long to put the fire out. We were so grateful that we had seen the tree. We patted one another on the shoulder, laughed, and were quite satisfied at our first success of the day. Then one of the firemen pointed up the mountainside. As my eyes went up the hill, my jaw dropped. We were so busy saving the tree that we lost the mountain.

The assistant fire chief walked up and slapped me on the shoulder. "You saved the tree, but you lost the mountain." Then I heard the voice of the Lord, "I did not call you to give eighty people a job in this town. I called you to publish the prophets. Your goal, your vision, and your focus must be that." Needless to say, it was a profound but very difficult lesson. The next day I would lay off twenty people, very painful indeed. But that vision saved the company.

CHAPTER 6

Where Do You Want to Live?

This is probably one of the most difficult chapters of this book to write. For it deals with the tendency we all have to decide God has either abandoned us or that we must find our own way. Even though we are certain God has called us, we are often unwilling to go through the heartache, the suffering, and the time that it takes to establish the work of the Lord. We forget that God's work is not just established in the earth, it is established in us as well. To be sure, if the work of the Lord is not established in us, it is difficult to see how His work can be permanently established in the earth. It is difficult—no, impossible—to separate the work of God from the character of the man or the woman. It is too easy to justify our actions, thinking we have the ministry in mind when we act or speak in a way the does not reflect the love of our Lord.

STAY THE COURSE

While it is true that our gifts flow in spite of our character, that is no excuse to live like hell while we work like Heaven. Ultimately, we discredit our ministry as we are personally discredited. How many times have we ruined our ministry by acting out some of the most torrid, fleshly attitudes in the Name of Jesus? But Paul said it best, *"…I show you a still more excellent way"* (1 Cor. 12:31).

We do have a choice. The question is simple: "Where do we want to live?" When we function in the gift realm, the gift flows freely since it flows out of us like water through a hose. But I do not want to live in the gift realm, which is the Holy Place. I don't want to be a hose through which the gift flows. I want to be a river, a well-spring flowing from Him who dwells from within the Most Holy Place of my heart. His seat is the Mercy Seat. His throne is my heart. Our heart is His seat of mercy. This kind of ministry flows from His character within us. He dwells in mercy and flows through holiness. This is the dimension that does only what the Father is doing. It is the dimension of all God—no showmanship, no ego, and absolutely no personal kingdom building. Ministering from this realm, one can truly proclaim, *"I can do all things through Christ which strengtheneth me"* (Phil. 4:13 KJV); *"for it is God who is at work in you, both to will and to work for His good plea-sure"* (Phil. 2:13).

Fruit that passes from generation to generation is fruit born of Christ Himself. Fruit that stands the tests of storms and time is fruit planted by Christ through folks yielded to Him and Him alone. This is where I want to live. It is where I strive to live.

REGRETS ARE PART OF GROWTH

It is easy to regret ever making an announcement to friends, colleagues, and other ministry folk that God has placed a call in our lives. It is easy to regret that we have made such incredible statements of faith, success, and hope concerning the vision that we have seen from the Lord. After the hype and excitement of the initial call begins to fade, the cold, hard reality of the work involved to bring it to fruition comes into view. Then you begin to understand the amount of work and struggle that it takes to bring real success to a God-breathed plan.

It is easy for us, and easy for our dreams, to go astray. It is easy for our understanding of God to take a hit during difficult times. We are challenged to the core. We are challenged to go a bit off course, to be just temporarily un-ethical, to wink at an unscrupulous opportunity. We justify these sidetracks by saying, "It is for the ministry, for the vi-sion God called us to." These changes give us the liberty to step away from the straight and narrow path of the purpose God has called us to, giving us the license to work in our own strength, to solicit support from those leaders in the flesh, to collect money according to the accepted ways of fleshly ministries who promise the world and deliver...another program.

You are hopefully reading this while saying, "This will never be me! I will never do that!" Praise God. Remember Peter:

> *From that time Jesus Christ began to show His disciples that He must go to Jerusalem, and suffer many things from the elders and chief priests and scribes, and be killed, and be raised up on the third day. Peter took Him aside and began to rebuke Him, saying, "God forbid it, Lord! This shall never happen to You"* (Matthew 16:21-22).

Then Peter denied Him.

Resolve is tested during the temptation. It is strengthened by the temptation. Resolve can never be assumed, for it can slip through your fingers before you realize what has happened. Stay small. Stay humble. Stay alert.

The ministries that are born of the Spirit of God and continue to be led by the Spirit of God are supported by the Spirit of God. But that does not exempt us from the difficulties of learning how to trust Him. It does not exempt us from the necessary growth and maturity. This growth is the process of moving from the realm where the gifts flow to the realm where Christ flows. The call of God does not mean that times will not be difficult. This is important for us to realize, or we will run to the methods of man and the carnal believer in order to fulfill God-breathed destiny. Where God guides, He provides. It's a nice little poem, but its reality goes deeper than we can imagine. Where God guides, He provides, and since He does provide, sweat is not required. Neither is badgering would-be supporters and softhearted believers into giving far more money than they can afford to give.

When the ministry does not take the time to allow God to build according to His plan and purpose, building by the flesh is the only recourse. And all of a sudden a vision born of God and the vibrant wind of the Holy Spirit is sustained by the sweaty, fleshly arm of humanity trying to prove to those around them that God is still in the midst of the vision. In the end, we merely slow down the progress of the supernatural lifestyle He has ordained for us.

He cannot work when we are clouding the spiritual atmosphere with our fleshly attempts to help God. Additionally, we tend to take the call He gave us into another direction that He is not leading, often assuming that success in one area automatically grants favor and success in another. Such an assumption slows our progress and limits our effectiveness in what we are called to do. In the end, after we take a few painful side journeys, we finally come to our senses and find ourselves far from where we should be. Then we need to expend unnecessary time, money, and strength to get back on track as we carefully take the time to hear His voice again.

He is always talking, but as we have seen, there are many things that will distract the heart that is not singly focused. Supernatural destiny is neither automatic, nor is it guaranteed. Its fulfillment requires our obedience, our holiness, and our brokenness. Folks with these qualities will most certainly change the world.

CHAPTER 7

God Sends
People to Encourage

*All the commandments that I am commanding you
today you shall be careful to do, that you may live and
multiply, and go in and possess the land which the
Lord swore to give to your forefathers. You shall remember all the way which the Lord your God has led
you in the wilderness these forty years, that He might
humble you, testing you, to know what was in your
heart, whether you would keep His commandments
or not. He humbled you and let you be hungry, and
fed you with manna which you did not know, nor did
your fathers know, that He might make you understand that man does not live by bread alone, but man*

lives by everything that proceeds out of the mouth of the Lord (Deuteronomy 8:1-3).

Brokenness and humility are essential to the work that God calls you to, no matter what that calling is. You can preach to tens of thousands in Africa. You can be on Christian television every day of the week. You can be father to three kids and work in a factory. You can be a stay-at-home mom preparing the next generation. Every job, every ministry, every profession is just as important as any other. Brokenness and humility are the keys to success in every area of life.

Are you aware of the blinding power of pride, personal ambition, and the need for success and recognition? Do you understand that where pride rules, humility cannot exist? Brokenness and humility help us to see clearly. They allow true spiritual discernment to operate in our lives. They help us to recognize those who want to walk beside us and assist us in our calling. Without discernment, the doors of our heart, our family, and our ministry are open not only to deception, but to those who would steal, kill, and destroy the very thing that God wants to accomplish through you. Many soft and encouraging voices will come alongside offering great encouragement, giving you unprecedented accolades, offering to serve you in even the most menial tasks. Although there are those who are genuine who can speak this way to you and offer that kind of a heart to serve, it is important that you be careful who you let inside the gates of your life.

My own pride blinded me to many situations that caused almost irreparable harm to me and the work. Even though there were those around me who warned me, primarily Cathy, I was unable to see what was right in front of me. After falling on my face many times over the years, I reluctantly began to understand that my need for approval and my driving desire to please my Lord caused me to believe people who should not have been trusted. Brokenness entered, did its job in my heart, and left me a better person.

Sometimes God sends special people who really have no ulterior motive but to love and befriend. Pastor Cleddie Keith from Heritage Fellowship in Florence, Kentucky, is one of those men. I met him in 1998 during the height of renewal and revival. We were at his church doing a video shoot of the miracles at his river meetings that are still held every Friday. This is one of the few places where God's manifest Presence is sustained. Our entire team worked endless hours to make sure that every aspect of the videotape was successful.

Upon returning home, I began to get phone calls from Pastor Cleddie. He told me he was praying for me; he asked me how I was feeling and always wanted to know if I needed anything. To me, he sounded just like many other men who contacted me out of a "deep concern" for my personal welfare. In reality, these folks wanted something from me. They either wanted money, a book published, my membership in their apostolic or prophetic organization, or a letter of approval to their constituency. I had grown weary of folks who simply wanted what I had but had no real concern for me. It is far better to simply tell a person what you want or need and be clear about your intentions. That kind of integrity and honesty is often, and unfortunately, too rare.

So after a year of receiving calls from Cleddie and speaking in his church, I wondered how soon he would drop the big question. He called me on a particularly difficult day. I was more blunt than I would normally have been; often my emotions get ahead of the proper way to relate to someone. I simply asked him, "Cleddie, what kind of a manuscript do you have to publish?"

"Why do you ask that?" he responded, "I don't have a book."

I was embarrassed and shocked. "Well, what do you need my help for?"

"I don't need your help for anything," he responded.

The conversation continued, and I found myself repenting before the Lord and to Cleddie. He was one of the few people who befriended me just to be friends. Here was a man with whom I could be real; with him, I could share my deepest secrets and my deepest pain. He understood the trials, the struggle, and the weight of international ministry. The more I got to know him, the more I realized that he is a true father in the faith. He possesses a genuine heart to see others advance to their fullest potential. Even though he is often in the background, he rejoices at the success of those around him. He is an encourager extraordinaire, a lover of God and his fellow man. He is one of those described by the writer of Hebrews, *"men of whom the world* [is] *not worthy"* (Heb. 11:38).

At that point in our relationship, I was able to let down my guard, and we became fast friends. To this day, I consider Cleddie the main pastoral influence in my life. Although he has published a few books with Destiny Image, they are books I had to encourage and almost pull out of him. Again and again he would say, "I'll go somewhere else to publish books; I just want to be your friend." Over the 12 years that Cathy and I have known Cleddie, we have found him to be a good friend, constant prayer support, and a powerful trumpet for the integrity and prophetic word we carry both personally and as a ministry.

Everyone needs a Cleddie in his or her life. Everyone needs at least one person who gives unconditional love with no pretense. We all need someone who genuinely has our best interests at heart, who is not afraid to be eclipsed by the one they care for, who is not interested in recognition, money, or the promotion of man.

Isaiah gives us an awesome picture of faith working through love in the Body of Christ:

> *Each one helps his neighbor and says to his brother, "Be strong!" So the craftsman encourages the smelter, and he who smooths metal with the hammer encourages him who beats the anvil, saying of the soldering, "It is good"; and he fastens it with nails, so that it will not totter* (Isaiah 41:6-7).

CHAPTER 8

A Miracle Takes Three Persons

It takes three people to make a miracle. The one needing the miracle needs to pray in faith. But there's always one who has to be obedient to make the miracle happen. Without this kind of co-labor and trust in the Body of Christ, most miracles will never happen. In fact, that's why many miracles don't happen, because there is not a willingness to trust the leading of the Holy Spirit among those the Lord wants to use. It is incredible to think about how miracles actually happen. God sees a need in a person. That person holds on to the faith that God will provide. The Spirit of the Lord then searches out someone who will be the answer to the need and moves that person to be the miracle that is needed.

I often wonder how many folks God had to speak to before He found the insurance man in Hawaii to be the other side of that $5,000 miracle I recounted in Chapter 4.

In everything I showed you that by working hard in this manner you must help the weak and remember the words of the Lord Jesus, that He Himself said, "It is more blessed to give than to receive" (Acts 20:35).

But I also often wonder how many times God calls on me to be the miracle in someone's life, and I do not respond, turning a deaf ear to the Holy Spirit. That thought gives me pause and makes me more determined than ever to give God His rightful place as King in my life. I want to be a giver that God can count on when the need arises. Of course, I have discovered that often God moves on my behalf even when I do not see my own need. God intervenes in order to move the ministry forward or to complete a task that I missed or messed up. Thank God for His watchful eye, His compassionate heart, and His undying desire to see His plan completed in me. It is indeed humbling to find that He has more faith in me than I have in either myself or in Him.

Such was the case early one morning when the Lord awoke me before my alarm clock: "You need to call the printer to cancel this run scheduled for today." I sat up in bed. Immediately I understood that it was the voice of the Lord. I called our production manager and asked her about the book that was scheduled for that day. My production manager said that a few steps were combined in order to meet a deadline. I instructed her to call the printers and hold the printing. Together with a proofreader, the production manager made the trek to the printing company to review the layout, pagination, and text of the book. Again, this was long before we had email, JPEGs, and digital readouts.

None of us were surprised when we discovered that several pages of the first chapter had been laid out incorrectly. This discovery saved us many days on our schedule as well as saving us from serious embarrassment.

Another time, an author was unable to pay for the books you purchase for several upcoming conferences. This particular author spoke often and was able to sell a consistent number of books per month. We had granted him credit, and up to this point, we had no problem. Now nearly nine months had passed, and although we were sending him books as he requested them, we still had not received a check, and he was far past due. Many phone calls and letters later, all the promises came to naught as we still had not received payment.

At the same time, the number of books we were publishing and reprinting was consistently on the rise. The cost of shipping the books from the printer grew along with the business. Our warehouse was growing faster than we had realized. On this particular afternoon, Cathy showed me the cost of having books shipped and recommended that we buy a truck in order to pick up our own books. That was a great idea, except that our business still had three mortgages, and 20 credit cards were the only guaranteed cash flow that we had. Even though we were spending $400 to $500 a month, we could not afford the truck we needed.

That same afternoon, while Cathy and I were in a meeting, the author who owed the money drove up to the front of our building. He walked in the front door and tossed a set of keys to my secretary. "Please give these keys to Don and apologize to him for me. This is the best I can do to pay the bill." He walked out of the building, jumped into the car, and drove away. My secretary came into my office and handed me the keys to a van. We then began to bring our own books back from the printer! God knows what we need before we know what we need. He knew I would extend more credit to this author than I should. He also knew this author was going to be unable to pay the bill. The truck was the perfect answer. I know what you're probably thinking, and it's a good question: Did the van cover his past-due amount? No, it didn't, but we could recognize a miracle when we saw it. So I marked his invoice "Paid in full" and sent it to him as a big thank you.

Then there was the time when we were called by a particular author to pick up the mechanicals and the production package of his book stored with another publisher who was about to go bankrupt. The publisher refused to cooperate by simply sending the material to the author. This author, who I only knew by reputation, asked me to make this six-hour drive for him as he lived on the West Coast. Jeff Newcomer, who has been a friend and co-laborer in Destiny Image from the very beginning, traveled with me everywhere I went at that time. We jumped into my 1979 Plymouth Horizon and headed toward New York. I should also add that this was early in February. The temperature was minus nine degrees with a 40 to 60 mph wind.

We knew the doors were closing on this publishing company for good on the day we got the word to pick up the materials. If we did not arrive before five o'clock, these materials would become part of the sealed inventory in the bankruptcy. It could be months or even a year or more before this production package would be released by the courts. We left early enough in the morning to give us four hours of leeway. Our expected arrival time was noon. But that cold wind was just a bit too much for that little Plymouth Horizon. Problem after problem hindered our trip as we tried desperately to get to the publishing house on time.

It was four o'clock in the afternoon. We were about 30 minutes away when our little Plymouth Horizon simply stopped running. Jeff Newcomer was driving. "I think she's finally died," I said to Jeff. He began to pull off to the side of the road, dropping the gear into neutral and hoping that the momentum of the car would get us safely off the highway. Then an amazing thing happened. Some could call it a coincidence, but I call it a miracle. The most incredible gust of wind you can imagine blew up behind us. After we pulled over to the side of the road, the car began to move forward on its own with the force of the wind. Jeff's first instinct was to put on the emergency brake, but I thought I was seeing the hand of God. I told him to release the brake and stay on the birm of the road. This amazing wind pushed that car along. Even more amazing was that we were headed uphill!

As the wind blew us along at approximately 5 miles an hour, we began to laugh, wondering if the wind would take us the rest of the way to the publishing house! We were in what appeared to be a very secluded, wooded area. Once we reached the top of the hill, much to our surprise, we saw a repair garage on the right-hand side of the road. "Turn in, turn in here!" I said to Jeff. He turned in and drove the wind-powered Horizon right into one of the stalls of the garage. The mechanics just stared as we drove by them. We sat there and laughed as we thanked God for His "personal touch" on our behalf. We simply jumped out of the car and told them it wouldn't run. Evidently, frozen fuel lines were a common problem that morning in the frigid weather, so that was the first thing they checked. They thawed the fuel line, added gas antifreeze to the gas tank, and off we went. We arrived at the publishing house as they were locking the front door. After a little bit of convincing, they opened the door and let us in. We signed off on the book materials and were able to bring them home to the author.

> *Now to Him who is able to do exceedingly abundantly beyond all that we ask or think, according to the power that works within us, to Him be the glory in the church by Christ Jesus to all generations, forever and ever. Amen* (Ephesians 3:20-21 NKJV).

MORE THAN I EXPECTED

One of the most profound statements the Lord spoke to us in the early days of preparing to open Destiny Image was that He would send us authors if we were faithful to the Lord. We had an uncanny awareness of the fact that God's hand was upon us, but also that He was watching. We knew that as we obeyed Him and allowed Him to guide us, we would see success. Of course—I must say this again and again—that does not mean that times will not be difficult, or that our faith will not be tried. God's hand provided more than miracles in the traditional, supernatural sense. God's hand also was a purifying hand. He corrected us, changed us, humbled us, and burned away the dross that we might be true representatives, not of doctrine, religion, or tradition, but of His prevailing life.

We discovered that the prophetic was far more than just learning prophecies or reading somebody's spirit. The true prophet had a lifestyle that reflected the life of God. The true prophet does not have to open his or her mouth to demonstrate God's life and love. In short, a prophet is as much who you are by character and Christ-likeness as it is what you say.

The hand of God working in and among His people is clearly an indication of the manifest reality of the miraculous, whether it is the wind pushing your car up the hill, or waking you in the middle of the night with an urgent supernatural intervention. If we had true spiritual eyes, we would see a continuous hovering of His angels protecting us and the Christ within us. If we could see the amount of spiritual activity occurring around us for our benefit, we would certainly have no doubt about who we are and what we are accomplishing.

Can you imagine being the president of the United States? The Secret Service is constantly going before you and following after you. They are above you and all around you. You are protected by people specifically trained to protect you at the cost of their own lives. Hidden in their clothing is an arsenal that would make a small country envious. Helicopters hover over wherever you are. Radar scans the skies in every direction while keeping in constant radio contact with the Secret Service on the ground. You are completely safe from harm.

Additionally, scores of advisors, diplomats, and assistants are feeding you information, advice, direction, setting schedules, clearing the way before you, and caring for your every need so you, as President, can be unencumbered in your focus on your duties as leader of the free world.

Therefore, we are ambassadors for Christ, as though God were making an appeal through us; we beg you on behalf of Christ, be reconciled to God (2 Corinthians 5:20).

But to which of the angels has He ever said, "Sit at My right hand, until I make Your enemies a footstool for Your feet"? Are they not all ministering spirits, sent out to render service for the sake of those who will inherit salvation? (Hebrews 1:13-14)

This same bustle of activity swirls around us every minute of every day. Just because we are not aware of it does not make it of no effect. Of course, seeing and hearing this activity would go a long way toward helping us cooperate with the Lord Jesus. We have no idea who we are or the lengths to which God goes to bring about supernatural destiny in our lives. Look, listen, wait. Heaven scurries with the activity ordained by your Father. You are in good hands.

> *For I am convinced that neither death, nor life, nor angels, nor principalities, nor things present, nor things to come, nor powers, nor height, nor depth, nor any other created thing, will be able to separate us from the love of God, which is in Christ Jesus our Lord* (Romans 8:38-39).

God, help us to understand who we are. Help us to see the reality of Your life and power within us. Let there be a true, clear demonstration of Your life on this earth. Your Kingdom come, Your will be done…in me. In Jesus' Name, open my spiritual eyes to things as they really are in Heaven and on earth.

> *Now when the attendant of the man of God had risen early and gone out, behold, an army with horses and chariots was circling the city. And his servant said to him, "Alas, my master! What shall we do?" So he answered, "Do not fear, for those who are with us are more than those who are with them." Then Elisha prayed and said, "O Lord, I pray, open his eyes that he may see." And the Lord opened the servant's eyes, and he saw; and behold, the mountain was full of horses and chariots of fire all around Elisha* (2 Kings 6:15-17).

But you are a chosen race, a royal priesthood, a holy nation, a people for God's own possession, that you may proclaim the excellencies of Him who has called you out of darkness into His marvelous light; for you once were not a people, but now you are the people of God; you had not received mercy, but now you have received mercy (1 Peter 2:9-10).

THE SALVATION OF THE LORD

But Moses said to the people, "Do not fear! Stand by and see the salvation of the Lord which He will accomplish for you today; for the Egyptians whom you have seen today, you will never see them again forever (Exodus 14:13).

Over the years, it has been remarkable to watch the number of men and women God would send to us. Many, many times the testimony was the same: "We never realized there was such a big difference in publishers. We had nearly signed with another publisher when God spoke clearly to us to publish with you." Every time something like this happened, it dropped the fear of God into us to a greater extent. We understood the mandate more clearly. We became more and more convinced that God's hand was on us. He was watching us. There was a specific responsibility that we carried to His people. The Holy Spirit showed us, *"...Touch not Mine anointed, and do My prophets no harm"* (1 Chron. 16:22 KJV).

But He showed us something that not many understand. All God's people are His anointed. The New Covenant priesthood is every believer. His anointing rests on everyone, not just an elite few. When the Lord says, "Touch not Mine anointed, and do My prophets no harm." The warning is to all men to respect and care for all believers.

For us, specifically, it was a joyful challenge to treat authors, bookstores, readers, and distributors with the same respect, honor, and kindness that we would normally grant to the most powerful of speakers. This kind of treatment extends also to the Destiny Image family. It extends to all those that have taken on the burden of this ministry in their lives. It includes the full-time people at our ministry center in Shippensburg, Pennsylvania, as well as those who have outsourced responsibilities around the country.

One of the greatest compliments we have experienced over the years is the feeling many of our people here at Destiny Image have expressed—that the work place is their church. They feel covered, cared for, respected, and trusted. This is not something we purposely set out to do. But as we have attempted to respond to God over the years, we realize the special nature of God's life and love upon all believers. We have discovered in real practical ways these Scriptures: "Do unto others as you would have them do to you" (see Matt. 7:12; Luke 6:31), and "Love thy neighbor as thyself" (see Matt. 19:19; Gal. 5:14). These are not just memory verses for children; they are life-giving principles to both the giver and the receiver.

More than 28 years have passed since Destiny Image first opened its doors. There is still a steady stream of potential authors who come to us by the leading of the Holy Spirit. I can't think of a more confirming sense than this. God is our marketing manager! We strive to be obedient, and the Lord sends us His people. He knows they will be loved and cared for. He knows that we will treat them the way we would want to be treated.

Nonetheless, it is important that you do not mistake meekness for weakness. For although God sends us authors all the time, the financial responsibilities and burdens of maintaining a company like this are often overwhelming. It is very difficult at times to respond to the Spirit of the Lord rather than to friends, good writers, and good messages that have every right to be published but do not fit in our genre of publishing or within the financial and production limitations of our staff.

At this writing, we receive over 3,000 manuscripts per year. We release ten new books every month. That means a lot of books are rejected. This is personally very difficult for me to do. There are often many books that could and should be published, but instead they receive a rejection letter. Some are turned down simply because we cannot possibly do every book that could be published. No matter how we word a rejection letter, it is still a rejection. I have a deep personal regret every time we have to send out one of these letters which, unfortunately, is quite often.

Because of our heart for the prophetic word and for His people, the urge to risk more than we should is also a constant temptation. I personally need to be certain daily that my pastor's heart and my calling in the prophetic are under His Lordship. If left to my own desires, I would most certainly limit, if not end, the very supernatural destiny God wants me to accomplish.

CHAPTER 9

Our Church Family

Supernatural destiny is called that for a reason. God intervenes in the lives of those He loves (that's all of us) to gather the resources, the opportunities, and the people to accomplish the destiny He has prepared. To recognize that God will bring people to you to help fulfill His plan is essential.

About a month before we started the business, and after we had announced to the church our intentions, a quiet young man approached me one Sunday morning. Jeff Newcomer was a servant's servant. His heart was and still is a powerful example of the heart of the Lord Jesus as a servant of all. Jeff made himself invaluable with not only his desire to serve, but with his wisdom and insight into the needs around him. Jeff could see a problem a mile away, and fix the problem before most people ever saw it coming along.

On this particular Sunday morning, Jeff approached me with something he said the Lord had spoken to him about. "I want to help you with Destiny Image. What can I do for you?" I was shocked and flattered, but honestly, I wasn't sure how I was going to feed my family, let alone provide a job for anyone else. Jeff then told me that he was laid off from his job and was available 15 to 20 hours a week to volunteer his services.

My father was a self-made man. He was an entrepreneur. He taught me many years earlier that you "don't let somebody work for nothing." He said that if somebody provides a service for you, that person needs to be paid. My dad said that it was only fair. He said he would not prosper on the back of someone else's sacrifice. *"For the Scripture says, 'You shall not muzzle the ox while he is threshing,' and 'The laborer is worthy of his wages'"* (1 Tim. 5:18).

But Jeff was insistent, telling me again and again that God had spoken to him. It would be several weeks before I relented and asked Jeff to help. But I knew that as soon as I could, I would hire him.

Jeff was a master of many trades, and what he didn't know how to do, he took the time to figure out. He turned out to be an invaluable asset in those formative years of Destiny Image. I don't know how we would have succeeded in making Destiny Image what it is today without his help. Jeff did what every true servant of the Lord does. He embraced the calling and vision that was on the Nori family as his own. Soon, he was not serving us, he was serving God. Everything he did, he did as unto the Lord and not to us or for us.

It is essential that business owners, pastors, and ministry leaders understand that principle; otherwise, it is easy to take on an air of pride and ingratitude. It's easy to move from an attitude of understanding that this man or woman is helping you and serving the Lord to an attitude of demanding condescension. When God sends help, He is sending Himself in someone else. Those folks need the respect and honor due them as servants of the Lord and carriers of the divine Presence. God sends them to take up where you lack. If we are too proud to accept their ministry, we dishonor them and the Lord. We will also find it hard to move forward without that person's work to take up where we cannot do what needs to be done.

Isn't it amazing how humility seems to be the key ingredient, the oil that keeps the wheels of God's plan moving?

Jeff also was instrumental in our work in the local church. The nameplate for his desk said, "deacon at large," and that he was. He could be a greeter, take up an offering, clean the bathrooms, lead worship, run the sound system, and shovel snow; anything that needed to be done, Jeff was ready and willing to do. He has always been and still is a shining example of someone who understands what it truly means to serve the Lord.

Now, thirty years later, Jeff Newcomer has not changed. He works quietly, efficiently, and diligently. He does whatever needs to be done, as always. In 1983 and 1984, Jeff carried boxes, delivered equipment, built an addition on our home that we used temporarily as an office, and kept our vehicles running. Now, these many years later, Jeff is still our "deacon at large," doing anything that he is asked to do, including travel with our international sales rep, Mary Moore, all over the world.

Cathy and I are convinced that we could not have found such a person as Jeff just by running an ad in the newspaper. I'm not even sure how I would have written his job description since I did not even know what I needed done.

BREAD OF LIFE FELLOWSHIP

I'm not sure what everyone in the church felt or thought when Cathy and I announced that we were starting a publishing company. We were a small, upstart fellowship of believers, a rather motley gathering of ragamuffins. We had little support from without, and not much depth within, as the congregation was mostly college students and recent graduates. Time and again we were told by those who knew better, "You can't build a church with college students. In fact, you can't do much of anything with university students." Although this kind of talk was prevalent in those days, it was most confusing. How could gifted leaders tell us one thing while we saw something completely different in our spirits? Of course, now I understand that this kind of talk is what causes one to be labeled a rebel, someone who simply does not submit to authority. It could be argued, however, that my desire was to submit to an authority a bit higher than a man-made, politically motivated authority. That's exactly what we did.

But in the early days of Destiny Image, the support from these ragamuffin believers was a sight to behold. None of us knew much about church planting. In a real sense, we were all just kids trying to live in the same house without any parents. We learned the hard way, by trial and error, and sometimes it wasn't easy. We shared meals often and spent a lot of time together. Cathy and I would often laugh that we were like Robin Hood and his Merry Men. But while Cathy was certainly a Maid Marian, I was more like Friar Tuck than Robin Hood.

Bread of Life Fellowship grew alongside Destiny Image Publishers; sometimes it was hard to tell the difference between the two. Most of the people that we fellowshipped with also helped in the business. There were many nights when much of the church came to the warehouse to help us pack books into the mailers or to help with the never-ending tasks surrounding a growing shipping department. We would often make an evening of it, bringing in pizza and games for the kids who always enjoyed being together while the adults worked. Of course, not everyone came out to help. Some had their own ministries; some were busy with other things. There was never coercion or intimidating comments to those who did not share the vision. We all must follow our own hearts, and we must all respect one another's decision as to how we spend our time. Jesus is Lord, not us.

...we are to grow up in all aspects into Him, who is the head, even Christ, from whom the whole body, being fitted and held together by what every joint supplies, according to the proper working of each individual part, causes the growth of the body for the building up of itself in love (Ephesians 4:15-16).

But we learned a lot together. We discovered that it was a whole lot easier to speak in tongues together than it was to work together. Iron sharpens iron, and sometimes iron beats against iron. Thank God, the love of Jesus always seemed to prevail! The children grew up to be close adult friends, and most of our relationships are still strong.

We have no doubt that our good friends and church family will share in the heavenly reward for their hard work and dedication to the Lord by serving Destiny Image and Bread of Life Fellowship.

Now he who plants and he who waters are one; but each will receive his own reward according to his own labor. For we are God's fellow workers; you are God's field, God's building (1 Corinthians 3:8-9).

CHAPTER 10

God's in the Small Things

I know it sounds crazy to say, or even think, that God needs to prove Himself to us. Nonetheless, there are times when you will question your calling. You question the very events that launched you on your journey. You will wonder if God really spoke to you. You will want to analyze and reanalyze all the circumstances surrounding your particular calling. You'll think about those people who approved of what you're doing and second-guess their motives. But most of all, you will question yourself. In my journey, I found these times very beneficial, but only in retrospect. While I went through them, it was an awful time of self-doubt and uncertainty.

Hard times usually set off these bouts of personal soul-searching. Difficulties will bring uncertainty; uncertainty breeds doubt; doubt breeds fear; and fear freezes the possibility of success in your life. It is good that we have a God who not only calls, but reaffirms. He not only calls and reaffirms, but He lays the path before us. It's not necessarily an easy or an inexpensive path, but He does make a way for us to accomplish what He has called us to do. The calling God puts on our lives still must be purchased with our own blood, sweat, and tears. It is a fact that inheritance passed on to the next generation is not appreciated nearly as much by the next generation as it is by the one who struggled to amass it. There is no question that something that you pay for is something that is cherished. God leads us into destiny, but He understands the need for that destiny to succeed. There is no doubt that the Lord will require us, as individuals, to take ownership of that thing.

> *Although He was a Son, He learned obedience from the things which He suffered. And having been made perfect, He became to all those who obey Him the source of eternal salvation* (Hebrews 5:8-9).

Think of it for a minute. Jesus is the Son of God. He was prophesied to be Savior and Lord. The prophets knew it; God knew it; the angels sang about it. Zacharias knew it, and his son was the prophet of the King. Mary carried Him in her womb, and she knew who He was. Nonetheless, Jesus learned obedience through suffering. All the prophecy in the world, all the faith you can muster, all the verses you can memorize will not bring you into your supernatural destiny if you are not willing to learn obedience the way Jesus learned it—through the things you suffer. We must understand that we are just like Peter. When the Lord Jesus told Peter to "feed My sheep," He saw Peter's inadequacy. But Jesus also knew that Peter would learn obedience through suffering, bringing him more completely into his own supernatural destiny.

> *Grain for bread is crushed, indeed, he does not continue to thresh it forever. Because the wheel of his cart and his horses eventually damage it, he does not thresh it longer. This also comes from the Lord of hosts, who has made His counsel wonderful and His wisdom great* (Isaiah 28:28-29).

It is not crushed forever, lest we lose heart. When God is at work in our lives, which He is all the time, He mixes a healthy dose of progress and success in the midst of the difficult times that are put in our path.

Such was the case with so many doors and opportunities the Lord opened to us as we were faithful to Him to the best of our ability.

Cathy and I worked out of our home for several months the first year of Destiny Image. It was 1983. But we were growing rapidly and soon had to attach a room to the side of our home. The company phone number, which we still have, was the home phone number we received when we married in 1973. I did not want to go to the expense of a new phone number and phone line until I was certain the cash flow was there to take care of it. It was not long before I was getting 20 to 30 phone calls a day. Cathy made the executive decision that it was time to get a separate telephone line for the business. Then, it wasn't long before we moved into a 5,000 square foot building, paying only four hundred dollars a month for it, including all utilities.

These gifts from the Lord were part of the continual affirmation we needed to keep going. We were convinced that we did not want to do something *for* God. The company needed to be born *of* God. If it was done at His direction, we would be co-laboring with Him instead of spending time doing something He had little interest in. In other words, we didn't want to build with wood, hay, and stubble, a sure sign of human effort resulting in humiliating failure.

Now if any man builds on the foundation with gold, silver, precious stones, wood, hay, straw, each man's work will become evident; for the day will show it because it is to be revealed with fire, and the fire itself will test the quality of each man's work (1 Corinthians 3:12-13).

We were so busy laying the foundation for the ministry that we didn't have a lot of time to look for buildings. But this was one of those times when God provided sovereignly. He reaffirmed to us in this tangible way that we were on the right path. Several years later, we noticed a 7,000 square foot building on 3 acres of land just off Interstate 81 in Shippensburg, PA. I wondered if it was something the Lord was giving us. Then one day as we drove by, the Lord spoke to

Cathy and me together, "This is your building." We were ecstatic. For the next year as we passed this building, we would hear the Lord saying the same thing. Rather than wonder where the money would come from, questioning the leading, or laying out a fleece, we simply said, "Yes, Lord, Your will, not our will be done."

The time came when our facility was just too small. I called on a realtor and told him the building I wanted to buy. "You've got to be kidding! I'm not going to sell you that property! You don't have the money for that price point! Do you know how much that costs?" He laughed, shaking his head, all the while reassuring us that there was no way we could buy that property.

Cathy and I left his office and looked at each other. Before I could say anything, Cathy looked at me, with full confidence, undaunted by this humiliation, and said to me, "We need to find another realtor."

We did find another realtor, and within three months we were in the building. By then, we had 30 employees. The office space was small, but the warehouse was sufficient. But it was only a few years before we again had severe growing pains. I designed the 12,000 square-foot office addition plus another 12,000 feet of warehouse space. But once again, the first few contractors I contacted laughed in amazement. "Do you realize how big this building is? You want to build that in Shippensburg? You can't possibly need that much space!" We simply found another contractor.

During all these growing pains, the Presence of God was ever near and dear to us. We knew we were on the right track as the doors continued to open. It also helped that there were so many people against it. We realized that those who questioned our abilities, our motives, and our hearts did not understand what it meant to carry a burden of the Lord. We knew we would need to take responsibility for our own actions. If we made the decision to build, it would be our decision alone. We would take the credit if it succeeded; we would take the blame, as well as the debt, if it failed.

We have discovered that there is nothing too small for the Lord. There is no detail that is unimportant. Every step, every decision is part of a carefully orchestrated plan so that the work has the international effectiveness God intends it to have.

But if God so clothes the grass of the field, which is alive today and tomorrow is thrown into the furnace, will He not much more clothe you? You of little faith! (Matthew 6:30)

There is a big difference between Olympic ice hockey and the kind of ice hockey we played as children in the frozen pond behind our home. One leads to a gold medal; the other leads to the flu. The two cannot even be compared. The more you work within your calling, the more you will care for every detail, and the more you will see God in every single step of the process. He never leaves you. He never takes a day off. He never takes a half-hour lunch break. He does not need health care. His hand is upon you persistently until everything He has dreamed for you comes to pass and has its full effect in time and space.

When I learn to focus on the Spirit, I increasingly see and understand the work of the Lord in my life. He is nearer than we can possibly imagine. He is more intimately involved with us than we can recognize with natural eyes. Recognizing this kind of divine involvement, even in the smallest details, makes it difficult to walk in uncertainty or unbelief. The children of Israel were within the consistent flow of the miraculous. God cared for them both day and night. He knew their needs. He knew how to feed them and how to protect them. He gave us the example of Israel for us to understand how He will be with us as He was with them. Such assurance is an invaluable moment-by-moment inner knowledge:

> *…that He who began a good work in you will perfect it until the day of Christ Jesus. For it is only right for me to feel this way about you all, because I have you in my heart, since both in my imprisonment and in the defense and confirmation of the gospel, you all are partakers of grace with me* (Philippians 1:6-7).

So the next time you want to worry about the details, step back, take a deep breath, and remember: God is in the small things too.

CHAPTER 11

Look for the Anointing, Not the Name

During that four-day vision back in the late summer of 1982, the Lord instructed me on what kind of authors to look for. The Lord said to me, "Look for the anointing, not the name." At first I had no idea what the Lord meant, but over time it became abundantly clear.

Not everybody with a national or international reputation seems to carry the Presence of the Lord. I'm not sure if it's personal charisma, good salesmanship, or good marketing that makes them successful, but one thing is for certain: There is a big difference between the popularity of one who carries the Presence and burden of the Lord and one who does not. One can be popular without the Presence of God, and one can have the Presence of God and no popularity at all.

God was very merciful to us. He gave us the ability to discern between the two. Over time, that discernment grew more and more keen. As a result, we have mostly been able to stay clear of those writers who did not accurately represent the Presence and power of the Lord. That is not to say that we only publish those who agree with us doctrinally. That is far from the truth. For we have also come to understand that within the Body of Christ there can be many views on the same Scripture. There can be many interpretations of the same doctrine. When I look for authors, I want the genuineness of true Christlike character, the reality of humility, and the peace of God. These kinds of people, although differing on some issues, are united in the centrality of Jesus in their lives and an absolute reliance on His mercy and power for success.

THE CARIBBEAN CALLS

In the early 1990s, Cathy and I were invited to Jamaica to do a writers' conference. We had never been to Jamaica before and did not realize how hot it was going to be there in August. Kingston was sweltering. I remember needing to shower three times a day just to be presentable before the people.

Our hosts, Dr. Peter Morgan and his wife Dr. Patricia Morgan, are gracious people. I cannot begin to tell you how much I have learned from them. They have been good friends and opened important doors for us. One of the speakers at the conference was a Bahamian preacher of whom I had no previous knowledge. As I heard him teach, I was so moved by what he said. I instantly knew that what he had to say was essential to the Body of Christ in the United States. I was happy to find out that he already had quite a large following in the United States.

The synergism of his popularity and our distribution network couldn't help but benefit both of us. Additionally, he spoke with the Presence of God and was respected by the Morgans and many others around the world. We had a great conversation, and a few months later we signed Dr. Myles Munroe. Thus began a long and fruitful relationship that continues to this day. Dr. Myles Munroe insists that God lives in the Bahamas and that it is most certainly God's country. However, after attending many of his August conferences in Nassau during the incredible heat of the Bahamas summer, I am not so sure who it is that lives in the Bahamas, especially in the summer!

THE POCONO CONNECTION

There was the time in the '90s that I attended an African-American women's conference in the Poconos in northeast Pennsylvania. The conference center was full, and the Presence and power of the Lord was very real throughout the entire building—such was the power of the main speaker. Below the main meeting hall was a corridor which was used for vendors to set up their various products. Everything from prayer shawls, Bible covers, anointing oil, books, and numerous other products lined either side of the corridor, leaving only a narrow space to walk from one end of the corridor to the next.

I was walking through this narrow space after the morning service when the main speaker began walking in the opposite direction toward me. I'm not sure who the bigger man was at that time, he or I, but one thing was certain, we were not going to easily pass by each other in that corridor. I did not know his name; he didn't know mine, but as soon as I got up to him, the Holy Spirit arose inside of me. I immediately stretched out my hand, placing it on his chest, and began to prophesy the wealth of revelation knowledge within him that would be turned into books. "You've got lots to say," I spoke to him. "You've got a book in you that is going to change the world." I realize that it may sound a tad disingenuous for a publisher to be prophesying a book out of a potential author, but you should know that this was not a normal event for me, specifically for that reason. I actually despise self-serving prophetic words. Well, to be honest, I despise any dishonest action that smells of flesh.

When I was done speaking to him, he politely shook my hand and smiled. After introducing ourselves to each other, I told him I was a book publisher. Then he asked me for my business card. About three weeks later he called me, and not too long after that *Woman Thou Art Loosed* by Bishop T.D. Jakes was published.

SUPERNATURAL INSTRUCTION

Early one morning as I drove to the office, the Lord and I were engaged in conversation, as we usually were. "Well, Lord," I began, "I wonder who I should contact today." It was more of a question to myself; nevertheless, the Lord heard me and very clearly said that I was to call Mahesh Chavda. I had met him many years earlier, but I had had no contact with him for a very long time.

So I stepped out in faith and gave him a call. You should remember that Destiny Image was not well-known for years. Those who did know us knew we were just a small, struggling company. We operated under the radar as we were not considered a very big threat to the industry. I had no interest in competing, anyway. The Lord had told me sternly during that first four-day vision, "You are not competing with other publishers. You are not competitors, but co-laborers." I don't know what others thought of me, but I knew for my part I was to keep my focus on the Lord, the goal, and myself. That kind of attention would keep me on track and small in my own eyes.

When I called Mahesh, he was as graceful and kind as I had remembered him to be in the mid 1980s. Mahesh and his wife Bonnie became fast friends of Destiny Image, and they are to this day. The Chavdas are one of those couples we are thrilled to publish. They are prophetic, strong in their faith, gracious, and filled with the love and power of God toward all.

At the end of the day, the only books that count are those that are God-breathed. These books bring hope to a dying world by showing the availability of God, as well as His healing, delivering power. His dreams for us are closer than we have imagined. His love is simple to experience, and He is committed to your personal salvation and success. Books that make these things attainable are the reason I get up in the morning. They are my motivation and my passion. For the Lord is near at hand; His salvation is close to those who simply call upon Him.

There are far too many examples of how the Lord has drawn men and women of anointing to Destiny Image. I know that it is the freedom we have given the Spirit of the Lord, as well as our commitment to Him in all we strive to accomplish, that has opened the doors to more than we can imagine. He is faithful even when we are faithless. He is near even when we do not sense Him. He is within us to work His good pleasure and His will.

> *At that time Jesus answered and said, "I praise You, Father, Lord of heaven and earth, that You have hidden these things from the wise and intelligent and have revealed them to infants. Yes, Father, for this way was well-pleasing in Your sight. All things have been handed over to Me by My Father; and no one knows the Son except the Father; nor does anyone know the Father except the Son, and anyone to whom the Son wills to reveal Him. Come to Me, all who are weary and heavy-laden, and I will give you rest. Take My yoke upon you and*

learn from Me, for I am gentle and humble in heart; and you will find rest for your souls. For My yoke is easy and My burden is light" (Matthew 11:25-30).

CHAPTER 12

A Lonely Journey

It is thought by many that the call of God will take them to new heights and exciting dreams of activity in the Spirit. Many imagine that a call of God automatically means popularity, many friendships, and visible success at every turn. But let me tell you what it is really like. The early days of supernatural destiny involve times of introspection, of a deep inner conflict of attitudes and actions that fight against the Presence of God in your life.

I have discovered that brokenness is a lifetime process. If your heart is open and you truly want to accomplish God's will, brokenness will be your companion for life. This is how it should be. For brokenness continually reminds us who we are apart from Jesus. Brokenness helps us keep our success in perspective. It continually reminds us of the pit from which we were removed, however many years ago. Brokenness is truly faithful in keeping our lives and our popularity under the Lordship of Jesus.

If you are honest with yourself, and if you allow honesty, repentance, and forgiveness to be part of your life, you will discover that brokenness comes alongside you as a very powerful safeguard against the temptations of the enemy and the words of those who would like to corrupt and deceive you. This fleshly activity will certainly corrupt the work that God has given you. The circumstances that brokenness leads us into will continuously point out places within us that require attention and, ultimately, repentance. We don't need sorrow or remorse; we need repentance. Brokenness is faithful to put us in situations that bring these fleshly roadblocks to light until we wrestle with them in the quiet solitude of our prayer lives. Brokenness knows that unless these personality issues, sin issues, and attitude adjustments are made, the end of our destiny is certain, and our lives end in shipwreck, sorrow, and much pain.

COVERED, BUT NOT CONCEALED

Personally, I am very conscious of my weaknesses. Regret is difficult to leave behind even after you repent. It is much easier for God to forgive me than it is for me to forgive myself. Many handle their weakness by denying it is there, by justifying it, or by construing a scriptural foundation for their sins. From personal experience, I know it is better to confess to the Lord who you are, what you are, and how you have failed Him. Honesty grants true forgiveness and releases His power to give you strength and freedom over the temptation. Because the gift seems to function in the midst of our weakness, we tend to assume that God does not care about the sin within. But as we all know, it will most assuredly mess up our lives, hurt our families, and throw up almost insurmountable roadblocks in our ministry.

When we do not cover up our sin before God, He will cover us. When we conceal our sin before the Lord, we leave Him no alternative but to uncover it, sometimes even before man. God's primary concern is for us as individuals. Brokenness strives to deal with the hidden sin. His goal is not to expose it to the world, although that is the inevitable end if we continue to conceal our sin before Him through one denial tactic or another.

> *When I kept silent about my sin, my body wasted away through my groaning all day long. For day and night Your hand was heavy upon me; my vitality was drained away as with the fever heat of summer. Selah. I acknowledged my sin to You, and my iniquity I did not hide; I said, "I will confess my transgressions to the Lord"; and You forgave the guilt of my sin. Selah. Therefore, let everyone who is godly pray to You in a time when You may be found; surely in a flood of great waters they will not reach him. You are my hiding place; You preserve me from trouble; You surround me with songs of deliverance. Selah (Psalm 32:3-7).*

BROKENNESS COMES

Brokenness will always come to you in the quiet of your own prayer life. He will speak to you concerning the issues of life. He will gently urge you to find a place of repentant sorrow and change. But we often ignore these early, quiet attempts to help us. God's mercy then enters and allows brokenness to put us into situations that expose our weakness in a very real way. The sooner we repent and turn from these unChristlike ways, the sooner we can go forward in fulfilling the destiny He has for us.

That is why I call this path the lonely path. For, much as we would like to say otherwise, there are very few people who will come along to whom you can bare your heart. There are few who will have your best interests at heart. Most are more concerned with carrying the news of your struggles to "faithful" intercessors who are only faithful at telling your secrets to the world. You need to know that the one or two folks who are honest with you are truly those who can pray for you, counsel you, walk with you, and cover you in prayer.

Many years ago, I had a preliminary diagnosis of cancer in my kidneys. I was told that if the tests came back positive, I would have but a few months to live. Devastated, I called my only very close friend in another state to get comfort, encouragement, and most of all, prayer. When I told him, he begged me for permission to tell his prayer chain. There was never any sense that he was concerned about me personally—no questions about how Cathy was doing or how my sons took the news. There was only his need to tell folks for prayer. Although prayer is necessary and a noble response, it was not what I wanted or needed at that point. He even called me a day later, again telling me he wanted to tell folks who would pray.

Thank God that the preliminary diagnosis was incorrect. Thank God that I had not told my family. I was fully prepared to tell them when the test came back, which I did.

I have a great team of intercessors who pray for me daily. They ask me for direction in prayer, and I desperately need that support. True intercessors know who they are, and they know that their very sacred ministry is done in the secret place of their prayer closets. I can and do tell them anything, and I can be certain that my needs go to God's ears only, as it should be. Thank you, Jeaniece, for being someone Cathy and I can count on!

But you, when you pray, go into your inner room, close your door and pray to your Father who is in secret, and your Father who sees what is done in secret will reward you (Matthew 6:6).

In the same way the Spirit also helps our weakness; for we do not know how to pray as we should, but the Spirit Himself intercedes for us with groanings too deep for words; and He who searches the hearts knows what the mind of the Spirit is, because He intercedes for the saints according to the will of God (Romans 8:26-27).

"For I know the plans that I have for you," declares the Lord, "plans for welfare and not for calamity to give

you a future and a hope. Then you will call upon Me and come and pray to Me, and I will listen to you. You will seek Me and find Me, when you search for Me with all your heart. I will be found by you," declares the Lord, "and I will restore your fortunes and will gather you from all the nations and from all the places where I have driven you," declares the Lord, "and I will bring you back to the place from where I sent you into exile" (Jeremiah 29:11-14).

DESTINY AND DIFFICULTIES

People are watching you. Some hope to see you fall, fail, or otherwise miss the mark. They are rooting on the sidelines...for your failure. I know this may be disappointing to some, even devastating, but it is true. The only thing some may see is the success. They may only see a person with a call on his or her life and the excitement that they assume surrounds that calling all the time. Deep inside, they want what you have, never realizing that God's dream for them personally is far more exciting and fulfilling than ours could ever be for them.

Most will not understand the trials and tribulations of those carrying the burden of the Lord—as though all people do not carry similar burdens. Everywhere I go and in everything I write, I make it abundantly clear that I am just like everyone else. I struggle with doubt; I face uncertainty. I have to deal with personal insecurity, evaluate my priorities, watch the finances carefully, and be sensitive to the Holy

Spirit so that I stay in the will of God. Believe me when I tell you that these are only a few of the things that I personally struggle with on a daily basis.

We could talk about health issues and the constant concern about my ability to work every day, to travel, to write, to be the husband and father I need to be. I could tell you about a heart attack, a stroke, neural sleep apnea, a birth defect, stenosis of the spine, and the list could go on.

Cathy and I have gone for years without close friends. The weight of the ministry and the burden of the daily responsibility consume your thoughts, your anointing, and your strength with the necessity of being completely focused on the path at hand. But that is the essence of what makes success in fulfillment of God's plan. For you, personally, the excitement is there daily and sometimes moment by moment. But the fear is often there as well. Fears regarding finances will keep you on your knees in prayer. The temptation to simply commercialize the message in order to ensure the finances is a real and credible temptation all the time. The focus on our personal calling is absolutely necessary. That must be at the forefront of all we do.

These things are extremely difficult to talk about. Very few understand the hardships and the uncertainty of pioneering something that has not been done before. But in sharing this with you, I am in no way complaining. Looking back over the years, these were very important, spiritually formative days where we learned the most essential lessons about life, ourselves, the Church, the business world, and the ways of our Lord. I want you to understand that supernatural destiny does not mean the absence of hard times. Even Jesus learned obedience through the things He suffered. When we are on the journey of life with our Lord, every day, every moment, every circumstance, offers an opportunity for growth and development.

Years ago, before I heard from the Lord concerning Destiny Image, I worked many jobs. Most of these jobs were hard manual labor positions. I managed a Kentucky Fried Chicken restaurant. I know, when you hear the word *manager,* you think of somebody sitting behind a desk ordering food and counting the money. But this was a working position. I didn't mind that, though. The physical exercise was good for me, and I enjoyed the hard work. What I did not enjoy was the prospect of spending the rest of my life cooking chicken for the little town we lived in. Many weeks were 70 to 80 hours of cooking, cleaning, and preparing food for our customers.

"Complaining" was a normal pastime for me in these days. Not because of the work, but because of the sense of destiny I carried in my heart. I often cried out to the Lord, "Lord, I was born for more than this. What is this burning in my heart? This is a good job; it pays well, but it is not why I was born." It took over a year before I realized that this restaurant was the school in which I would learn a lot about business. One busy day as I was preparing chicken and complaining, I said to the Lord, "Lord, I am going to die making chicken for Shippensburg. I will go through my whole life, and I am going to be known as the chicken man." Then I saw a most devastating picture in my spirit. It is funny in retrospect, but very real at the time. I saw my tombstone. On the front of it was carved a big chicken drumstick. My epitaph read, "Here lies Don Nori. He gave Shippensburg a good piece of chicken."

It was an awful thing to see. "Oh my Lord, I was born for more than this." At this point, I really began to understand what God wanted to teach me: I was not alone. I was not forgotten. He said to me in a very quiet and very powerful voice, "Every job you have is preparing you for what I have for you. Your life is a school in which you will learn the details of how to run a business as well as how not to run a business." As you can imagine, I was quite shocked at this discovery but immediately began the process of repenting. Daily retraining my mind not to be a complainer but to be thankful was difficult at first. But I remained diligent to accept where God had me. For the first time in my life I could rest, knowing that I was in His hands. I did not have to strive, intercede, or worry. I knew, deep inside, that at the right time, He would move me on.

Soon, and I know this is hard to believe, I began to enjoy the process. I became attentive to the Holy Spirit. I knew that the best way to move on from the restaurant was to learn what I needed to be taught. I actually began to hear the voice of the Lord more clearly. I realized that for me that restaurant was the fire in which those things that would hinder me for the rest of my life were constantly being exposed.

I actually began to love the fire. This fire is not exactly the fire we pray for when revival comes along. It is not the kind of fire that millions of people fly over the ocean to experience—but it is the fire that purifies the soul and strengthens resolve. It is this kind of fire that prepares those who will most certainly change the world.

> *Blessed be the God and Father of our Lord Jesus Christ, who according to His great mercy has caused us to be born again to a living hope through the resurrection of Jesus Christ from the dead, to obtain an inheritance which is imperishable and undefiled and will not fade away, reserved in heaven for you, who are protected by the power of God through faith for a salvation ready to be revealed in the last time. In this you greatly rejoice, even though now for a little while, if necessary, you have been distressed by various trials, so that the proof of your faith, being more precious than gold which is perishable, even though tested by fire, may be found to result in praise and glory and honor at the revelation of Jesus Christ; and though you have not seen Him, you love Him, and though you do not see Him now, but believe in Him, you greatly rejoice with joy inexpressible and full of glory* (1 Peter 1:3-8).

CHAPTER 13

Handing Over the Torch

When our son Donald was just over a year old, he began having seizures. Doctors told us that the bone that is supposed to cover his brain did not cover it completely. There was a triangular-shaped hole right at the top of his head. The doctors gave him test after test after test. There was no indication that it would ever close. The prognosis we had for him was that he would be wearing a helmet until his head closed—possibly for the rest of his life. We left the doctor's office that Friday afternoon devastated. We cried out to God for help. Sunday morning we called for the elders of the church to lay hands on him and pray for him. The next day we went into the doctor's office so he could be fitted for a helmet. When they did the X-rays to determine exactly how to build the helmet, they discovered that the hole had closed. God had intervened supernaturally.

Early one Sunday morning, Donald walked into our bedroom and announced that he had seen Jesus. "An angel came to me last night," Donald said to us. Of course Cathy and I both jumped up out of bed to hear what happened. "Well, it was Jesus," Donald said. "And He told me that my heart was all dirty and that I needed to ask Him to take away the dirtiness and to be sorry for my sins." "And...and..." We prompted excitedly. "I told Him I wanted Him to live in my heart and that I was sorry for my sins, and then He just climbed right into my heart." Well, Kathy and I were dumbfounded; what he had experienced was amazing! I sometimes see myself as quick and brash as Peter often was. My response to him was simply, "Donald, that's great. The next step is to be filled with the Holy Spirit and speak in tongues." Donnie looked at us and laughed. "Dad, I already do that." "You already do that?" "When Jesus came into my heart, He told me He wanted me to pray like you and mom and the other angels pray, so I started to pray in another language." Again, the supernatural intervention!

Probably one of the most incredible miracles of Donald's life is that he lived long enough to give his heart to Jesus. Donald was mischievous to put it lightly. Kathy was convinced that he never slept. She would often say to me, "That boy just sits up all night making plans on how he's going to make my life miserable!" When Donald came into our room to announce that Jesus was now living in his heart, we never realized what would happen. His life truly changed. Donald the troublemaking, mischievous one was now the arbitrator, the friend, the softhearted companion, the protector. He didn't get counseling; he didn't get time-outs; he didn't sit in the corner. I didn't lecture him; the boy just got saved. I know some of you may think he was too young to get saved, while others would say he had reached the age of accountability. All we know is that one day he was a demon disguised as our son, and the next day he was an angel disguised as our son. His vocabulary, his actions, and his life changed. Call it what you want, but it was a mirror role of God's intervention.

I could go on and on concerning the mirror goals that we have seen in our lives. Our fourth son Joel had his broken arm healed by the Lord. Stefan, our youngest, literally fought with a spirit.

Then there was the time our oldest son Jon, at the age of 12, got the bad news that he needed to have braces. With a surge of faith, I told him that I would pray for him, and instead of needing to wear braces for four years, they would come off in just a few months. Every day I would put my hand over his mouth praying in tongues and commanding that the teeth be straightened out. I never lost faith; every day I prayed for him…every day for five years until the braces finally came off. He didn't seem negatively affected by that until our middle son Matthew needed braces. He announced at the dinner table that he would need braces for four years. Jonathan instantly spoke up and said, "Don't let dad pray for you; you may never get rid of them!" I don't know why it happened, but I prayed for Matt every day just as I did for Jon, and instead of needing braces for four years, they were out in four months, and his teeth were perfect.

ARGUING WITH THE LORD

A few years ago, I realized that I would not live long enough to do everything that I knew was on God's heart for the ministry. It was a humbling realization. I felt like a failure. I asked the Lord to forgive me, to help me. I was frustrated at the amount of time I had wasted missing the leading of the Holy Spirit.

In the midst of my self-flagellation, I heard the Lord deep in my spirit. I did not expect it, didn't ask for it. I was in the middle of a self-gratifying pity party when the Lord Jesus interrupted me: "You do not understand." I tried to argue; I really did. "Lord, I failed You. You gave me this fantastic opportunity, and I blew it." When the Lord spoke to me in 1982, He spoke of the publishing company, satellite television, and movies; in fact, He spoke of a media engineering company to "engineer the media to the purposes of God." But after all these years, the only thing I had accomplished was publishing the prophets. I know that that is a major accomplishment, but when you put it in perspective with everything I heard those four days, I had failed. So when the Lord told me I did not understand, I tried to argue with Him. I blew it, plain and simple.

Thank God, He is more persistent than I am! "No, you do not understand!" He said again. I figured it was time to keep quiet and listen, so I did. I know that discovery. It is generational! Cathy and I are doing what we are called to do so my sons and their children and their children can do what they need to do. Incredible!

For years, our sons were part of the business. We began early to teach them the business. They learned the publishing industry from the bottom. They started by sweeping the floors, packing books, shoveling snow, and cleaning the bathrooms. They answered phones, delivered books, and sold books at conferences. I took one son with me every time I traveled, which was often. They learned book manufacturing procedures, bookkeeping and accounting, author relations, and the all-important sales processes.

All the while, they saw their parents at their best and certainly at their worst. They learned to forgive, repent, and ask God for wisdom by watching their mom and me in the crucible of daily life and ministry. They learned to hold onto their faith, their integrity, and their family by walking through some extremely difficult times with us. They know the uncertainty of finances and the fear of near bankruptcy, as well as the tenacity of moving forward in spite of overwhelming obstacles. They watched us stand when everything within us wanted to run. They saw us cry out to God when so many "friends" stood against us. They learned the loneliness of the burden with us and sacrificed alongside of us. They earned their place in Destiny Image every bit as much as we did.

So when I understood that God was calling the family, I was relieved that Cathy and I had our sons at our sides for many years. This is not to say that the transition to the next generation of leadership is simple, for it absolutely is not! After all, we changed their diapers! We fed them bottles; we taught them to talk, ride a bike, and hit the pot when they went to the bathroom! It is not hard to remember all those times when you are turning your life's work over to these same kids. It is extremely helpful to see that they carry the same mandate as you do; they see it, feel it, and understand it.

My last major handoff to them was the design of the covers. Although I still have responsibility for content, they are now caring for all aspects of the ministry. But I have to be honest and tell you that of all the difficult pieces of the business to turn over to them, the cover art was the hardest. After a particularly difficult cover meeting, I was, once again, complaining that "these kids have no idea what constitutes a good book cover." I said to the Lord, "I do not think I will ever be able to move out of this area. They just do not get it!" That was one of those complaining moments when I neither expected nor asked for a response from God.

Nonetheless, once again I stood corrected. "I never called you to run an old man's company."

"What? Who's an old man?"

"I never called you to wrestle creativity into your own design paradigms and antiquated processes."

Well, that was, as they say, that. It was so clear, so obviously God, that I had to turn the creative reins over to a generation prepared to take them.

I have learned a very important lesson. I need to stick close to the primary issue of my calling...content! "Publish the prophets!" is my mandate. "Get the word out however you can. Open new doors. Discover new ways. Don't allow small thinking to hold you back! Your identity is in Me, not in what you do." These points have been, and still are being, burned into my spirit. If I stay true to my calling, I make room for my staff to function in their callings. I no longer have to dominate and control what happens. I have prepared my sons. I have full confidence and trust in their ability to hear the Lord and make right decisions. We still discuss issues, weigh options together, and look for new opportunities together. But the execution is on their desks. I give them a wide berth, however, as we have experienced sustained growth even in the midst of tough economic times. Now I am free to be and to do what is in me. I have waited nearly thirty years for this time to come. Thank God for His love, mercy, leading, and grace.

By age 28, our son Donald was running the largest family-owned, full-Gospel Christian book publishing company in the world. Jonathan, at age 31, was by his side in a solid leadership team along with Nathan Martin, another thirty-something who has bought into the work. Our 26-year-old son Joel is an attorney and is expanding Destiny Image with a major motion picture company called Destiny Image Films. Our first full-length movie, *A Christmas Snow*, was released in October of 2010, after winning first prize for best film at the XP Media Film Festival. As the next generation takes flight, the continued fulfillment of the vision takes flight with them.

Cathy and I could not have imagined what has happened with Destiny Image and our sons. We kept ourselves focused day by day on working the business and raising our sons as best as we knew how.

> *Now unto Him that is able to do exceeding abundantly above all that we ask or think, according to the power that worketh in us, unto Him be glory in the church by Christ Jesus throughout all ages, world without end. Amen* (Ephesians 3:20-21 KJV).

CHAPTER 14

What Is Supernatural?

Miracles come in all shapes and sizes. They come in all forms and descriptions. They are simply the supernatural intervention of God into the lives of humankind. Whether that intervention is visible in time and space, or only detectable in the spirit realm, miracles happen minute by minute all around us. The sooner we develop eyes to see what actually is happening in the spirit, the sooner we can take comfort in His constant care and supernatural activity in our individual lives.

There is no doubt that obvious divine interventions are exciting. I have seen the hand of God intervene in my life and family more times than I can possibly remember. I could probably write a book on the miraculous things that we have seen happen over the years. However, it is also true that these times of supernatural, clearly visible, divine interventions were few and far between. For a long time, we lived with the notion that if we could not see a verifiable intervention of God, there were no miracles taking place in our lives. We believed that God only worked supernaturally in times of crisis and great need—or when I simply made a mistake, and He was left to correct the mistake by Himself. This kind of thinking meant that much of the time we felt very much alone. It made us feel as though we had to accomplish most of what we were called to do in our own strength, in our own wisdom, and with the very limited resources that we had at the time.

But thank God for preceding revelation. Thank God that He continually opens Himself to us that we may understand Him and His ways more clearly. The Bible is full of verses on learning to hear the voice of the Lord, on understanding that His ways are not our ways. The wisdom of God is greater than the wisdom of man. It is unfortunate, however, that we only seem to understand these verses as a result of the brokenness that we endure.

The things I'm going to tell you now I wish I had learned many years ago. It would have made our lives much easier. We would have lived with a greater sense of joy and anticipation. But you have an opportunity to learn from our struggles. If you take these things to heart, your journey will truly be one of joy even in the midst of hardship.

GOD'S HAND STAYS

Now when the attendant of the man of God had risen early and gone out, behold, an army with horses and chariots was circling the city. And his servant said to him, "Alas, my master! What shall we do?" So he answered, "Do not fear, for those who are with us are more than those who are with them." Then Elisha prayed and said, "O Lord, I pray, open his eyes that he may see." And the Lord opened the servant's eyes, and he saw; and behold, the mountain was full of horses and chariots of fire all around Elisha (2 Kings 6:15-17).

In your darkest times, when God's voice seems nonexistent and His Presence is nowhere to be found, He is still there. Not only is He still there, He is still working on your behalf and on the behalf of your family and those around you. Elijah cried out, "Lord, give him eyes to see what I see!" The mountains were filled with the armies of the Lord.

Lord, give *me* eyes to see what You are doing around me. May my spiritual perception grow and develop that I might be able to see Your hand of mercy, healing, restoration, guidance, love, and persistence on a moment-by-moment basis.

I'm not going to pretend to tell you that I know why God's Presence seems so distant at times. Sometimes it feels as though He has lifted His hands from us. But I can say with certainty that His ways are not our ways. He will never leave us or forsake us. As Moses declared so many years ago to the children of Israel, *"He brought us out from there in order to bring us in, to give us the land which He had sworn to our fathers"* (Deut. 6:23). God doesn't change His mind halfway through a plan. He does not give up, quit, or take a holiday. We do those things, but He does not. Ever.

That was the hope that carried Cathy and me for many years. We knew that what God did for Israel, He would do for us. He did not call us out from the life we had into the wilderness of struggle and uncertainty just to send us back to where we came from as though none of these incredible things had happened. He brought us out to bring us into our destiny. Although the wilderness never seems like it, the wilderness is the highway to destiny. Therefore the wilderness itself is your destiny. Without taking that road, you will never step into what God has called you to. Of course, once you enter your promised land, you will find that it is full of giants that also must be conquered. But at that point, you are certain of what you are fighting for! That battle never seems to end, but what you gain is the sustained sense of His Presence and the knowledge that He is in charge. When you are certain of God's never-failing, never-ending love, you can do anything. *"...He Himself has said, 'I will never desert you, nor will I ever forsake you'"* (Heb. 13:5).

Sometimes Cathy and I were so singularly focused on the particular thing that God had given us to do that we failed to recognize all that He was doing in our family. We failed to recognize that God was speaking to our children, our neighbors, our friends. While we may be blinded to our own influence, those who are benefiting from that influence are being changed all the time. We realized that when we thought God had abandoned us it was because we did not always see the flashing red lights of verifiable miracles in front of us. But the true reality of His gentleness, compassion, and nearness is contained in the fact that He is carefully and lovingly at work in the hearts of all those we hold dear.

He turns the hearts of the children to the father (see Mal. 4:6). That's a miracle. He calls upon husbands to love their wives as Christ loves the Church; that's a miracle (see Eph. 5:25). He admonishes children to obey their parents in the Lord, for this is good (see Eph. 6:1). He promises parents that if they will train up their children in the way they should go, they will not depart from it when they are old (see Prov. 22:6). That is certainly a miracle. These and many, many other verses prove that the hand of God is at work in us and those around us. While we see the work of the Lord develop, if we open the eyes of our spirit, we will also see how God's hand builds the lives of those for whom we pray.

The lesson we learned was a hard one. When we are alone, we are not alone. When we don't feel the hand of God, His hand is still there. When we think God is off taking care of another crisis, His eyes are still upon us. He still lives within. We are not a spiritual bed & breakfast, where the Lord comes and goes depending upon our faith, actions, and attitudes. God is not fickle! He is focused, determined, and tenacious. He is so big He can give each one of us 100 percent of His attention. He's got a one-track mind, and He can dedicate His one-track mind to each of us personally.

We are never alone. We are never forgotten. He never gets tired of us. He never takes a break from us; He never withdraws Himself. He is always at work to will and to work His good pleasure (see Phil. 2:13). For we are His workmanship, created in Christ Jesus for good works (see Eph. 2:10). He will never leave as orphans (see John 14:18). He doesn't forsake us (see Heb. 13:5). The most profound understanding of His love recognizes that He is near even when we have failed, made a mistake, or forgotten to pray. He is bigger than we are. He is not controlled by fleshly human emotions and self-centered desires. He is steady, single-minded, and determined to bring us to Himself.

SEE THE SUPERNATURAL

So we must redefine what we call the supernatural activity of God. Those who look at God's supernatural activity as only the physically verifiable activity of God on earth miss so much. The greatest miracles are a change of heart, a change of attitude, a redirection of purpose, the discovery of destiny. We are not just human beings having a spiritual encounter. Quite the opposite is true. We are spiritual beings having a human experience. Our lives are supernatural in every way—whether it is the miracle of a changed attitude or a check in the mail from an unknown source. Understanding this fact changes your life from a dreary life of waiting for an occasional miracle to a life of wondrous discovery as you watch the hand of the Lord moving continuously all around you.

CHAPTER 15

Laborers
in the Harvest

Sacrifice and offering Thou didst not desire; mine ears hast Thou opened: burnt offering and sin offering hast Thou not required. Then said I, Lo, I come: in the volume of the book it is written of me, I delight to do Thy will, O my God: yea, Thy law is within my heart (Psalm 40:6-8 KJV).

Supernatural destiny seldom happens alone. The principle of the Body operating in unison is prevalent throughout Scripture because it is a foundational principle for success in any endeavor. Low rules rarely find true and lasting success. Supernatural destiny is a Body affair. It blossoms and grows as the vision is caught naturally, purely, genuinely, and enthusiastically by those who have a heart for the work. No amount of coercion, guilt, or fear can create this godly desire in someone when it is not naturally born.

GOD SENDS VISIONARIES

I never get tired of watching new staff members genuinely capture the vision for what God has called Destiny Image to do. As in all walks of life, there are those who will work for you because it is simply a good job. There is nothing wrong with that. I am happy to have people who are there, working hard because it is a good job. They may have no vision for what we're doing, but they have a vision for caring for their family and want a good, permanent place to work. I thank God every day for these people, because I know God sent them to us.

Then there are those who carry the burden of the Lord. They are the ones who go home at night and still carry the work in their hearts. They pray and open their hearts to the Holy Spirit all the time on the behalf of the ministry. This is not something that is required or expected, but it is common among those who carry Destiny Image in their hearts and understand they are a part of something bigger than themselves that is changing the world.

DO YOU SEE WHAT I SEE?

There is nothing more exciting than genuine revelation. When Jesus asked the disciples who they thought He was, He was ecstatic over Peter's response: *"Simon Peter answered and said, 'Thou art the Christ, the Son of the living God'"* (Matt. 16:16 KJV).

Pure revelation goes straight to the heart. It changes the mind. It builds faith. It gives destiny, purpose, and a reason to live. There are few things more fulfilling than coming to the realization that God Himself is speaking to you. This God-breathed communication changes a person forever. It cannot be faked, and it certainly cannot be ignored. When He shows Himself to you, the profound change from within will make you a different person for the rest of your life.

This is far different from being called by man. When God calls, there is a sense of freedom and liberty. When God calls, you become part of something because God has placed it in your heart.

It is unscriptural, unfair, and fundamentally unchristian to expect your employees to work far more hours than they can physically endure; to work weeks or months without pay because the money isn't there; to be expected to put the ministry before their family—and all, of course, in the name of the Lord. Employers like this will not live in the fullness of God's blessing. They will be able to access the system, and as the children of Israel did in the wilderness, they will have enough to survive, but not enough to prosper. True spiritual (and financial) prosperity is not a result of claiming Scriptures or holding weekly fasts and all-night prayer meetings, etc. It is the result of honoring God and His people, both those who work for you, and those you expect to give their hard-earned money so you can continue in the ministry. It is amazing that we will do almost anything to beg God to provide for us rather than simply trusting Him and properly caring for His people.

Those who know the Nori family well can easily tell you that we are not perfect. We don't claim to be. But one thing we try to do is respond to God and His ways to the best of our abilities without ignoring His principles and presuming His blessing. In this way, the hand of the Lord can continue to be on us in mercy, grace, and success. We are painfully aware that without Him we are nothing.

In addition to being our marketing manager, it has always been exciting to see that God is also our human resources director. Supernatural destiny requires special people to do God's work. You cannot simply hire friends, neighbors, and ministry associates to do the work God has called you to do. Although it is true that some folks you already know may end up working with you toward your supernatural destiny, we have discovered that, since the destiny is supernatural and the work is primarily an undiscovered land, only God really knows who can do the jobs needed to bring about His plan.

Over the years, I have been mistakenly credited with much more of the success of Destiny Image than I really deserve. Cathy, my wife of nearly 40 years, has carried the burden of the work of the Lord in her heart from day one. Pregnant with our fourth child when God first spoke to us to publish the prophets, she was energetic and excited about the call God had placed on our lives. Over the years, she has filled many roles in my life. She is my wife and best friend, the mother of our five sons, business partner, counselor, homemaker, pastor's wife, and prophetic intercessor. That's a lot of hats for one person to wear; Cathy has worn them well. She is the best at moving in and out of projects, major problems, research and development, and day-to-day management of the company.

There were several years when I was very sick. I had a concussion, which led to neural sleep apnea, waking seizures due to the trauma of the concussion, stroke, heart attack, and spinal stenosis. During these years, I was unable to function for more than a few hours a day. Cathy led the charge to help care for the needs of Destiny Image while caring for me as well. I will never be able to thank her enough for her willingness to lay aside her own hopes and dreams in order to step in and continue to build Destiny Image along with our older sons, who delayed their university training in order to help Cathy. Through this very difficult time, Destiny Image continued to grow and develop. The family carried the work in their hearts. They knew the Lord they served. They had seen the principles of His life demonstrated in Cathy and me. No one will ever know how difficult these years were for the whole family. We worked hard, prayed hard, and cried hard. Sometimes we even laughed hard!

As for me, I didn't know whether I would ever be able to return to work full time. I struggled with a sense of failure; I fought depression. I watched Cathy and my sons changing their futures as they went into the office every day while I spent many hours at home trying to understand what was happening.

For Cathy and my sons Jon, Don Jr., Matt, and Joel, it was an extremely difficult time. Endless hours of work multiplied by an increased weight of responsibility as the company continued to grow tested their limits on a daily basis. All of that was combined with the uncertainty of my health. At one point, doctors told Cathy that they did not know how long I had to live and that I should get my house in order.

But Cathy continued to prove to be the dedicated warrior that I always knew she was. She was unwilling to accept the doctors' diagnosis. She started the most critical research and development project she had ever undertaken. That project was to find a way to bring me to health. Even though the Internet was in its infancy, Cathy spent hours online researching symptoms, talking to her sister who was an ER heart nurse, and calling specialists around the country. She made the diagnosis of neural sleep apnea, called a neurologist, and asked for an appointment. The doctor's response was disbelief. Sleep apnea was a condition that very few people even knew about, let alone understood. Cathy found an out-of-state doctor who had a very primitive sleep lab for overnight sleep apnea testing. He discovered that she was correct. Needless to say, the treatment began immediately, and 15 years later I am still here, back at work, and enjoying both Cathy and the work God called us to do.

But God sent others to us as well. In fact, sometimes people just seemed to appear out of nowhere. An old house church leader of Cathy's teenage days, Dick Woodcock, came into our lives once again when we started our business. He just happened to be an established Christian book salesman independently selling books for many publishers up and down the East Coast. His counsel, prayer, love, and advice through some extremely difficult times was truly a miracle. Only eternity will show what this great man, our personal hero, did for the work of the Lord. We are certain that he is now looking down from Heaven and is part of the great cloud of witnesses cheering us on.

Still others helped carry the burden. The work of the Body of Christ cannot be overestimated. The work that the Lord brings in is too big for one person, and often it's too big for one family. Such was the case with us. Such is the case for all those who carry destiny in their hearts. Do not be afraid to share your vision. Do not feel jealous when others carry the burden with you. Do not get protective. At the end of the day, the credit is not what is worth it. What is important is the success of the work of the Lord. The more you allow God to add to your foundational staff, the more you will grow. The more you honestly trust them with responsibility, the more they will shoulder the weight that such a destiny carries. There are some who say that my original health problems began because I did not understand the necessity of Body ministry. Whether that is true or not I do not know, but I do know I have learned the absolute necessity of sharing the work, the responsibility, the benefits, and the accolades of the work of the Lord.

I would be remiss if I did not mention others whom the Lord has used over the years to carry the weight of responsibility. Don Milam, who is now our senior author representative, has been with us for 15 years. His work, love, dedication, and belief in Destiny Image Publishers have helped spread word of our integrity all over the world. He has been and continues to be my good friend. He is a co-prayer warrior, confidant, and laborer for the work of the Kingdom of God. Merlene Rill was with us for twelve years. She served as my personal assistant, director of research and development, and later as general manager of the company. Together with Cathy and my sons, she helped to navigate us through the most difficult and trying times of the business.

Bob Vanderbreak, Allen Knight, Stefanie Flewelling, and many others also came at the leading of the Lord and carried the burden of the ministry. All those who came alongside us, even for a season, are part of the success of Destiny Image, and we are grateful for their labor among us.

> *Therefore encourage one another and build up one another, just as you also are doing. But we request of you, brethren, that you appreciate those who diligently labor among you, and have charge over you in the Lord and give you instruction, and that you esteem them very highly in love because of their work. Live in peace with one another* (1 Thessalonians 5:11-13).

With the Wind Under Our Wings

Do you not know? Have you not heard? The Ever-lasting God, the Lord, the Creator of the ends of the earth does not become weary or tired. His understanding is inscrutable. He gives strength to the weary, and to him who lacks might He increases power. Though youths grow weary and tired, and vigorous young men stumble badly, yet those who wait for the Lord will gain new strength; they will mount up with wings like eagles, they will run and not get tired, they will walk and not become weary (Isaiah 40:28-31).

There is no clearer mandate from Heaven than the one you personally hear for yourself. There is no greater certainty than knowing that no matter who you are, where you have been, how you have failed, or what your perceived drawbacks are, God has dreamed about you. He has dreamed the most exciting and fulfilling future for you. He is holding it in Heaven for you till the time that you simply say, "Yes, Lord, I want all You have for me." Then He releases the power of Heaven to bring that dream into your reality.

Just as a bride says "yes" to her lover, without exactly knowing what is ahead of her, so your "yes" says much the same thing: "I love You. I want to spend eternity with You!" The future is not clear, but you are certain that love will carry you through together. Whether the times be good or bad, you are certain of your trust in Him. You are certain that He only wants the best for you. Your adventure begins at the very moment you agree with Him. Only time will unfold the magnitude of your commitment to Him. Only eternity will show you how redemption was effected in the earth due to your obedience.

Only God knows the depth of His love and desire toward you; He has dreamed for your life.

Supernatural destiny is intended for everyone—personally, completely, and finally. There is no doubt that God has prepared it for you. There is no doubt that He unleashes the very powers of Heaven to bring it to pass. There is no one else He is more interested in than you. He is so-o-o big (that's right!) He gives all His desire and attention to each one of us individually.

The world is different because you were born. It can be better because you have determined to walk with God. This is your time in history.

About the Author

Don Nori, Sr. has authored fourteen books and has worked in the publishing industry for more than 25 years. He has ministered internationally for more than two decades, working with people of all races and nationalities. Don and his wife of 38 years, Cathy, live at the foot of the Appalachian Mountains in south central Pennsylvania where they raised five sons and now also enjoy their daughters-in-law and grandchildren.

Don Nori, Sr. is the founder of Destiny Image Publishers. Don spends most of his time writing and ministering internationally.

- Visit Don Nori, Sr.'s Website for itinerary, video blogs, and new books: www.donnorisr.com.

- View his Youtube videos at: www.youtube.com/donnorisr.

- View daily posts and interact with him on Facebook: Don Nori, Sr.

- Check out his radio show, "The Prophetic Edge," every Friday at 11:00 A.M. EST www.blogtalkradio.com/donnorisr.

- If you would like to contact him regarding a speaking engagement, please email him at donnorisr@gmail.com,

- or contact his assistant Alex Sadowski at 717-532-3040 ext. 124 or ams@destinyimage.com.

In the right hands, This Book will Change Lives!

Most of the people who need this message will not be looking for this book. To change their lives, you need to put a copy of this book in their hands.

> But others (seeds) fell into good ground, and brought forth fruit, some a hundred-fold, some sixty-fold, some thirty-fold (Matthew 13:8).

Our ministry is constantly seeking methods to find the good ground, the people who need this anointed message to change their lives. Will you help us reach these people?

> Remember this—a farmer who plants only a few seeds will get a small crop. But the one who plants generously will get a generous crop (2 Corinthians 9:6).

EXTEND THIS MINISTRY BY SOWING
3 BOOKS, 5 BOOKS, 10 BOOKS, **OR MORE TODAY,**
AND BECOME A LIFE CHANGER!

Thank you,

Don Nori Sr., Founder
Destiny Image
Since 1982

DESTINY IMAGE PUBLISHERS, INC.

"Promoting Inspired Lives."

VISIT OUR NEW SITE HOME AT
WWW.DESTINYIMAGE.COM

FREE SUBSCRIPTION TO DI NEWSLETTER

Receive free unpublished articles by top DI authors, exclusive

discounts, and free downloads from our best and newest books.

Visit www.destinyimage.com to subscribe.

Write to: Destiny Image
                P.O. Box 310
                Shippensburg, PA 17257-0310

Call: 1-800-722-6774

Email: orders@destinyimage.com

For a complete list of our titles or to place an order
online, visit www.destinyimage.com.

FIND US ON **FACEBOOK** OR FOLLOW US ON **TWITTER**.

www.facebook.com/destinyimage   **facebook**
www.twitter.com/destinyimage   **twitter**